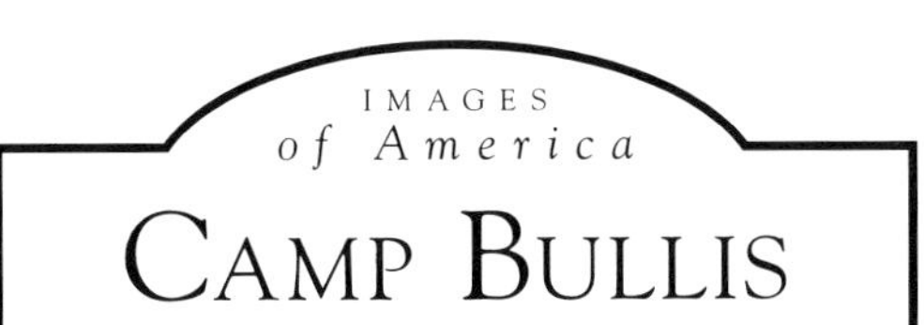
IMAGES
of America
CAMP BULLIS

After service in the Civil War, Capt. John Lapham Bullis established a reputation as the most successful Indian fighter in history. He led the Seminole-Negro Scouts from 1873 to 1881, participating in 25 field operations, including seven cross-border operations. In 1917, the 90th Division at Camp Travis named the encampment at the Leon Springs Military Reservation as Camp Bullis. (Fort Sam Houston Museum.)

On the Cover: As a noncommissioned officer signals "follow me," his squad advances with fixed bayonets. This charge took place during the Proposed Infantry Division Test in 1937 at Camp Bullis. A combat veteran might advise this squad not to bunch up so much, even though this makes a better picture. (Fort Sam Houston Museum.)

John M. Manguso

ISBN 978-1-4671-2749-3

Published by Arcadia Publishing
Charleston, South Carolina

Printed in the United States of America

Library of Congress Control Number: 2017940506

For all general information, please contact Arcadia Publishing:
Telephone 843-853-2070
Fax 843-853-0044
E-mail sales@arcadiapublishing.com
For customer service and orders:
Toll-Free 1-888-313-2665

Visit us on the Internet at www.arcadiapublishing.com

This book is dedicated to the soldiers, sailors, airmen, and marines who trudged the dusty trails and soldiered at Camp Bullis. Hell's Fire and Fuzzie-O!

Contents

Acknowledgments 6

Introduction 7

1. A Good Range Is Essential 11

2. The Leon Springs Military Reservation 21

3. A Cinematic Interlude 39

4. Preparing for the "Big War" 49

5. A New Mission 73

6. Admirably Suited to All Purposes 105

About the Organization 127

ACKNOWLEDGMENTS

The images in this volume appear courtesy of the Fort Sam Houston Museum (FSHM), the US Air Force Security Forces Museum (USAFSFM), the US Army Medical Department Center of History and Heritage (ACHH), the Library of Congress (LOC), and the Defense Visual Information Distribution System (DVIDS). For their help preparing this book, I thank Gary Boyd and the other historians at the US Air Force Air Education and Training Command; Rudy Purificato and Ken Neal at the US Air Force Security Forces Museum; Carlos Alvarado at the US Army Medical Department Center for History and Heritage; Todd G. White and Charles Patrick Howard at the 502nd Air Base Wing, Joint Base San Antonio; and Paul Dvorak and Timothy Plummer at Joint Base San Antonio–Camp Bullis. The introduction is drawn largely from "Camp Bullis: Admirably Suited to All Purposes of Military Training," a monograph written by this author for the Army in 1990.

Special thanks go to Carl Ekmark, who left a 30,000-image record of activity at Fort Sam Houston in the 1930s. I would also like to thank Mrs. Dunmire, my first history teacher, for getting me interested in history; Dr. John K. Mahon, my advisor in graduate school at the University of Florida; Brig. Gen. Joseph P. Kingston, who gave me my job as military history detachment commander; Maj. Gen. Henry Mohr, chief of the Army Reserve, who advised me to "tell it like it is, even if no one believes you"; Maj. Bennie Boles, who hired me as a museum curator at Fort Sam Houston; Col. Jim O'Neal, Ed Miller, and Ron Still, three of the best supervisors a museum director could have; Joan Gaither, whose support as president of Preservation Fort Sam Houston has been invaluable; and Caroline Anderson, my title manager at Arcadia Publishing, who kept me focused and gave encouragement throughout the preparation of this book. Special thanks go to Jacqueline Davis, who has been my strong right arm for most of my 33 years at the Fort Sam Houston Museum.

Most of all, I thank my beloved wife of 50 years, Barbara, whose support has been and continues to be priceless.

Introduction

Fifteen miles north-northwest of San Antonio, Texas, lies Camp Bullis—almost 30,000 acres of rugged, hilly terrain. Here, American fighting men and women have practiced marksmanship and tactics for more than a century. This patch of land initially grew out of the needs of the troops at Fort Sam Houston to fire their weapons safely and maneuver tactically. When the small garrison of fewer than 200 men at the post at San Antonio moved to Government Hill, about two miles from the center of town, in 1879, there was plenty of open land near the post where the soldiers could maneuver and fire their weapons without endangering the populace. But San Antonio was growing, and so was the garrison of the post. The post soon had the second-largest garrison in the country. It was no longer safe to fire weapons on post. In 1886, the War Department purchased a 310-acre tract farther out of town for a rifle range and maneuver ground. It was three miles from the post, on the north side of what became the Fort Sam Houston National Cemetery.

This worked until San Antonio grew into the area to the north and residents complained of stray bullets landing on their property. As early as 1890, soldiers from Fort Sam Houston had leased tracts of land near Leon Springs and Kerrville, Texas, for firing ranges and maneuvering. Various terrain studies and reconnaissance were conducted by the Headquarters, Department of Texas, to identify an adequately sized tract of land for purchase. The search was interrupted by the war with Spain in 1898, but the aftermath of the war made the acquisition of training land imperative. Fort Sam Houston was to become a brigade post, making it the largest Army post in the country. It was not until December 1, 1906, that any purchase was made. On that date, the War Department purchased the Oppenheimer and Schasse Ranches near Leon Springs, plus four small parcels around the periphery, aggregating some 17,273 acres.

Units at Fort Sam Houston used this area, the Leon Springs Military Reservation, periodically for training, but no major improvements were made except to lay out five campsites and some firing ranges and to dig wells to increase the water supply. The first large-scale maneuvers at the Leon Springs Military Reservation took place in 1908. During the Maneuver Camp at Fort Sam Houston in 1911, some 12,000 troops maneuvered at the reservation. National Guard units mobilized for border service in 1916 also trained there.

After the declaration of war on Germany in 1917, the Army leased an additional 15,427 acres of land south of the reservation. This tract extended the southern boundary to the intersection of Lockhill-Selma Road and the San Antonio & Aransas Pass Railway. The additional land was required to support the training of the 90th Division and other units mobilizing at Camp Travis, adjacent to Fort Sam Houston. On the Scheele Ranch in this tract, a camp of tents and temporary buildings was established on September 12, 1917. The camp was designated as Camp Bullis by 90th Division General Order No. 84. It was named for distinguished Indian fighter Brig. Gen. John Lapham Bullis. On the western portion of the reservation was Camp Stanley, a collection of cantonments for the training of officer candidates, cavalry and artillery units, and the Signal Service. Camp Stanley was named in War Department General Order No. 134 in 1917 for Brig. Gen. David S. Stanley, who was awarded the Medal of Honor in the Civil War and commanded the Department of Texas from 1884 to 1892.

After the First World War, the Army relinquished most of the leased land but made a permanent expansion of the reservation by adding 4,543 acres with purchases between 1920 and 1933. This included the land occupied by Camp Bullis. Camp Stanley was converted into an ammunition storage and processing facility. Land totaling 1,760 acres was transferred to the Chief of Ordnance in 1933 and 1937. Another 2,244 acres would be transferred to Camp Stanley in 1953 and 1970.

In the 1920s, the Army allowed the Leon Springs Military Reservation to be used for the filming of the motion pictures *The Rough Riders*, *Wings*, and *The Big Parade*. *Wings* won the first-ever Academy Award for Best Picture in 1927. Troops from the 2nd Division at Fort Sam Houston and the 5th Cavalry Regiment from Fort Clark served as the proverbial cast of thousands for these productions.

Facilities at Camp Bullis were developed to support the field and tactical training of the 2nd Division as well as the Citizens Military Training Camps (CMTC), the Reserve Officer Training Corps (ROTC), and the Organized Reserves. Many of today's cantonment buildings and the swimming pool were constructed in 1930 and 1931.

From 1937 to 1939, the 2nd Division conducted field tests at Camp Bullis to develop a streamlined division structure more suitable for mobile warfare. These tests led to the adoption of the "triangular division," which was the standard Army division during World War II and the Korean War. When war erupted in Europe in 1939, the Army began to mobilize. To accommodate an increase in the number of troops in training, Camp Bullis was expanded again in 1941 by extending its eastern boundary to Blanco Road and acquiring land along Cibolo Creek in the north. These accessions added 10,306 acres to the reservation. An additional 7,000 acres north of the Cibolo Creek were leased for maneuver areas.

During the Second World War, three infantry divisions and numerous smaller units used the ranges and training areas at Camp Bullis. New facilities constructed during the war included a prisoner-of-war camp, two mock villages for combat-in-cities training, a fortified area as a stand-in for the Siegfried Line in Germany, several new and expanded ranges, and facilities for the Provost Marshal General School. To optimize the use of the available space while accommodating the greatly increased number of troops and weapons systems, the firing ranges were redistributed around the edge of the reservation, firing into a central impact area. Problems with tick-borne disease late in the war led to a curtailment of some large-scale training activities.

By the end of World War II, the size of Camp Bullis was no longer adequate to accommodate the size, firepower, and mobility of an infantry division. The flight paths of San Antonio International Airport passing over Camp Bullis restricted artillery firing, and by May 1949, all artillery and mortar firing was terminated. Consequently, Fort Sam Houston's mission changed from a garrison for a combat division to a medical training center for the Army when the US Army Medical Field Service School and the US Army Medical Training Center moved to Fort Sam Houston. This, in turn, led to a change in the nature of the facilities at Camp Bullis. Weapons firing and maneuvering yielded to combat medic training and medical field service, though many units continued to use Camp Bullis for small arms firing, land navigation, and tactical training.

Soldiers from the Medical Field Service School and the Medical Training Center became the principal users of the camp during the Korean War. By 1954, the Medical Training Center had a full-time presence in the cantonment area. Air Force trainees from Lackland Air Force Base and Reserve Components soldiers were also frequent users. Army Special Forces began communications and medical training here in 1952. In October 1956, Air Police training was transferred to Lackland Air Force Base. This added yet another major customer for Camp Bullis.

Facilities continued to be improved, and additional areas were developed for specific types of training. The cantonment area at this time could house 500 trainees in framed tents. These would soon be replaced by hutments built on concrete slabs. Trainfire ranges were added in 1960. Black Jack Village was developed specifically for the training of combat medics. Medical training alone in 1962 amounted to 99,262 man-days of activity. The sound of helicopters was heard in the training areas as trainees practiced aeromedical evacuation. The Vietnam Village was erected to prepare soldiers for service in Vietnam in much the same way the mock villages were used during the Second World War. Camp Bullis was also the test site for the Medical Unit, Self-contained, Transportable, or MUST. This modular system could be configured into any type of hospital facility depending upon the number and types of modules assigned to it.

As the war in Vietnam wound down, so did activity at Camp Bullis. In view of this, the size of the military reservation was reduced. Some 323 acres were transferred to the City of San Antonio and became Dwight D. Eisenhower Park, opening in 1988. Another 94 acres would be transferred to Bexar County in 1977 to allow the widening of Blanco Road, and 47 acres were turned over to the county for a park.

Greater reliance on the Reserve Components in the post-Vietnam era saw increased use of Camp Bullis by the Army Reserve and National Guard. In 1975, an armory and maintenance facility was built at Camp Bullis for units of the 49th Armored Division, Texas National Guard, that were stationed at Fort Sam Houston.

The Airbase Ground Defense Course was established at Camp Bullis in 1974. To support this activity, the Air Force Security Police Training Site, known as Victor Base, was constructed in 1977 near the Schasse Ranch. The Air Force was the largest single user of Camp Bullis until 1987, when the Air Base Ground Defense School moved to Fort Dix, New Jersey.

With the creation of the Emergency Deployment Readiness Exercise, or EDRE, Army units from around the country began to use Camp Bullis for training. The EDRE required a long-distance movement followed by a tactical exercise. Use of Camp Bullis gave a more realistic field exercise, away from familiar and well-used home station training areas. Some notable EDREs included a battalion from Fort Campbell, Kentucky, preparing a drop zone between Pike and Butte Hills in February 1980. The 82nd Airborne Division parachuted units into this drop zone later in the year. In 1985, the 307th Medical Battalion and a French army medical unit dropped into Camp Bullis, and various units from Fort Hood also conducted EDREs here.

A combat assault landing strip, or CALS, was built in the northeastern part of the reservation in 1983 to support joint air-ground training that involved the Army, Air Force, and Marines at various times. The 1st Marine Amphibious Force landed at the CALS in 1986 and 1989 for exercises at Camp Bullis.

After the DEPMEDS (Deployable Medical System) was introduced, a training site for this system was established in 1987. This system replaced the MUST as a mobile hospital. A suite of DEPMEDS equipment was located here to train Active and Reserve Army, Navy, and Air Force medical units that were being equipped with this system. DEPMEDS was first used in combat during Operation Desert Shield/Storm in 1991. In addition to the drop zone and CALS, Camp Bullis added a hospital clinic, an armored personnel carrier assault course, a land navigation course, and the Intelligence Training Army Area School.

In the 1990s, Camp Bullis was used by active Army, Army Reserve, and National Guard units mobilizing and deploying to Southwest Asia for Operations Desert Shield and Desert Storm as well as for subsequent operations in that region. Other units were subsequently deployed for operations and training exercises in the Caribbean, Central America, and Europe. The Air Force Airbase Ground Defense School returned in 1995. Warrior Week, a tactical exercise that exposed the security forces trainees to a realistic expeditionary experience involving survival skills, basic field hygiene, and force protection situations, was added to the curriculum in October 1999.

After the attacks on the World Trade Center in New York and the Pentagon in Washington, DC, on September 11, 2001, units and individuals deploying to Afghanistan, Iraq, and elsewhere in support of the Global War on Terror trained at Camp Bullis. To facilitate this, a mock forward operating base, FOB Courage, and mock village typical of the Southwest Asia theater of operations were constructed, continuing a 60-year tradition.

Following the 2005 Base Realignment and Closure Act, the Department of Defense began to transfer the training of the enlisted medical personnel of the Navy and Air Force to Fort Sam Houston, joining with the Army Medical Department Center and School to form the Medical Education and Training Campus. This brought the number of medical trainees of all services training at Camp Bullis to 45,000 annually.

Today, Camp Bullis offers not only traditional maneuver areas and small arms firing ranges but also a fully instrumented urban assault course, the fully instrumented Combined Arms Collective Training Facility, and a live-fire "shoot house." There are drop zones for parachute operations; the Combat Assault Landing Strip, which can handle C-130 aircraft; a convoy tactical simulator; a convoy live-fire range; a demolition range; hand- and rifle-grenade ranges; nap-of-the-earth flight routes; and a chemical, biological, radiological, and nuclear training area, including the traditional gas chamber.

In addition to its strictly military usage, Camp Bullis has other uses as well. Under the Army's "multiple land use" concept, the reservation has been used by Boy Scout and Girl Scout organizations. In addition, federal, state, and local law enforcement officers use the small arms ranges. And the Department of Energy has conducted exercises here as well. Some 27,000 acres of Camp Bullis are under agricultural grazing leases. Parts of the reservation are held as easements by the San Antonio River Authority and the Alamo Soil Conservation District for the operation of the Salado Creek Flood Control Project. Some 27,000 acres can be used for hunting during the state-designated hunting seasons. The whole reservation is managed as a habitat for numerous wildlife species, both game and nongame, including the endangered golden-cheeked warbler and the black-capped vireo. Skillful management allows these birds and soldiers to coexist. Camp Bullis balances its diverse military training requirements and land management practices through a process called Integrated Training Area Management. This program considers the amounts and types of training, the extent of the training areas and facilities, the natural and cultural resources on the reservation, and the land maintenance and rehabilitation measures required to ensure no net loss of training and mission requirements.

The Army at Camp Bullis built relatively few permanent structures. The camp headquarters (built in 1917) and many of the cantonment buildings (built in the 1930s) are, despite their ages, "temporary structures." The oldest buildings predate the Army's arrival. Family quarters are clustered around the original Scheele ranch house. Several of these buildings were moved here from the other parcels of land that were added to the reservation. The Panther Springs Ranch complex is another noteworthy grouping of buildings. In addition to these historic structures, there are numerous prehistoric sites. On the other hand, troops training at Camp Bullis now have access to a Burger King restaurant and a well-stocked post exchange shoppette.

In 1891, Brig. Gen. David S. Stanley stated the need for a maneuver area and firing range for Fort Sam Houston. Since its initial purchase, the Leon Springs Military Reservation has grown in size to 27,993 acres and in the number and types of facilities on it to support the changing needs of the armed forces. The land acquired has proven to be very adaptable to those needs as the Army changed from a foot- and horse-mobile force armed with black-powder firearms to a modern force equipped with motor vehicles and aircraft, armed with powerful individual and crew-served weapons, and aided by high-technology systems to support tactical operations, logistics, training, and administration. The variety of the terrain, the amount of land, the year-round good weather, and its easy access from local posts and bases contributed to its adaptability to a wide variety of uses. The ability of the Leon Springs Military Reservation to accommodate changing military needs over a period of more than a century confirms the wisdom of the selection of this piece of land as admirably suited to all types of military training and bodes well for the continued use of Camp Bullis through the 21st century.

One

A Good Range Is Essential

Like most professions, that of the soldier requires practice to maintain proficiency. For the small garrison in San Antonio, this was not a problem. At first, the soldiers set up a backstop behind the officer quarters for marksmanship practice. Tactical training could be done in the unoccupied land around the post. As the garrison of the post became the second-largest in the country and the population of San Antonio grew, more space was needed to do this safely. A plot of land about three miles to the north was purchased in 1886. Here, the troops could fire their rifles and conduct maneuver training. Soon, however, San Antonio grew into the area around this piece of ground, too, and complaints about stray rounds endangering civilians and livestock forced the Army to move its training and weapons firing farther from the post. Brig. Gen. David Stanley noted in his 1891 annual report that a good range was essential to an Army post and that the post at San Antonio was in sore need of one. Thus began a 15-year-long search to identify an area where the garrison could fire its small arms and artillery and maneuver safely and economically. The search ended with the purchase of the Schasse and Oppenheimer Ranches near Leon Springs in 1906. Here, the Army would begin to develop the necessary training facilities on the Leon Springs Military Reservation. Within two years, the Army would conduct large-scale maneuvers involving the regular Army and the National Guard. This reservation was used extensively for maneuvers during the 1911 Maneuver Camp and during the mobilization of the National Guard after Pancho Villa's raid on Columbus, New Mexico, in 1916.

The garrison of the post at San Antonio, a mix of cavalry, infantry, and artillery, drills on the Lower Post Parade in the late 1880s. Only small numbers of troops could use the target range behind the officer quarters. There was insufficient acreage for infantry or cavalry maneuvers, and artillery firing was out of the question. (FSHM.)

In 1886, the Army purchased this piece of ground three miles from the post for a rifle range and maneuver ground. The firers are using a position suitable for long-range firing. The second soldier at each firing point coaches the firer and keeps score. Behind the firing line, the tower serves as an observation post for officers to insure safety. (FSHM.)

Artillerymen from Light Battery L, 2nd Artillery, perform crew drill on a 3-inch Ordnance Rifle at what would become Fort Sam Houston. The two men in front of the gun insert and ram the projectile while the sergeant aims the gun. The man to his right thumbs the vent. This cannon could fire a projectile 4,100 yards. (FSHM.)

The garrison of Fort Sam Houston, with a regiment of infantry, a battalion of field artillery, and a regiment of cavalry, totaling almost 1,800 soldiers, was too large to maneuver on the 310 acres purchased in 1886. The 4,000-yard range of its rifles and the 8,000-yard range of the new breech-loading artillery were too great to permit firing them in an area only 2,400 yards wide. (LOC.)

Camp Bullis lies within the Edwards Plateau. The terrain is rugged and hilly, as seen in this view from the cantonment area to the north. Many streams course through the area, the principal ones being Salado Creek, Cibolo Creek, and Lewis Creek. Streams are intermittent in nature, existing as dry streambeds during most of the year. (FSHM.)

Most of the hills are rocky, like Butte Hill, and do not support vegetation. Along the valleys of the major streams, a loamy soil exists to a sufficient depth to support excellent vegetation. Overall, the soils will not support crop production but are adequate to support grasses for grazing livestock. Cedar, cactus, and live oak abound within the reservation, offering some concealment. (FSHM.)

Stone walls like these were often used to mark the boundaries between ranches. Compare these groups of infantry soldiers in position behind these stone walls as they perform completely different tasks, even though both are similarly armed. Above, the soldiers are practicing marksmanship. The focus is on proper shooting technique. The other group is acting tactically, the men concealing themselves behind the wall. Unlike the marksmanship group, they are fully equipped with cartridge belts, haversacks, and blanket rolls—items that would disrupt their aim on the range. Another difference is their hats. The marksmanship group has its hats creased fore and aft. The tactical group sports the Montana peak style. Around 1912, the Montana peak became the standard, dating this picture later than marksmanship group photograph. (Both, FSHM.)

Battery C, 1st Field Artillery, dashes across an open field with its gun sections abreast during the summer of 1908. At that time, the Leon Springs Military Reservation was hosting its first tactical maneuvers. These involved regular Army troops from Fort Sam Houston and other posts, as well as National Guardsmen from four states. (FSHM.)

Infantry soldiers take up firing positions along the side of a road through the Texas countryside. At the left of the firing line are two M1904 Colt-Maxim machine guns. Before the purchase of the ranchland that would become Camp Bullis, the Army would rent tracts of land for field exercises and weapons firing. The original of this image is a color postcard postmarked 1909. (FSHM.)

A machine gun section is pictured with two guns deployed into a firing position. Placed on the reverse slope of a small rise, the guns can fire over the top of the rise while minimizing their exposure to return fire. The pack mules that transport the guns and ammunition are also sheltered from return fire. (FSHM.)

Soldiers from the 18th Infantry trudge up one of the many dusty trails at the Leon Springs Military Reservation. This regiment had come from Fort MacKenzie, Wyoming, to participate in the Maneuver Camp at Fort Sam Houston in 1911. After marching from Fort Sam Houston, the regiment took part in tactical maneuvers around Leon Springs. (FSHM.)

On the way to Leon Springs in 1911, this column from the 15th Infantry Regiment trudges along a dirt road. Trailing the column are the pack mules carrying the unit's water-cooled Colt-Maxim machine guns and their associated tripods, ammunition, and water cans. This trip usually included an overnight bivouac, but some units could cover the distance with full packs in less than 12 hours. (FSHM.)

The 1st Illinois Infantry Regiment was mobilized for border service on June 26, 1916, and assembled at Camp Wilson adjacent to Fort Sam Houston. Here, the regiment's 3rd Battalion holds a formation next to its lines of pup tents at Leon Springs. Mustered out in October, the regiment was called up in 1917 and served in France with the 33rd Division. (FSHM.)

A battery of M1902 field guns conducts live-fire service practice. To the left of each gun is an ammunition caisson containing a mixture of high explosive and shrapnel shells. This type of field gun could fire a 3-inch-diameter, 15-pound projectile out to a range of 8,000 yards. (FSHM.)

This group of soldiers trains as artillery forward observers. They observe the impact of the shells fired by the battery. They will calculate the deviation in direction left or right of the target and whether the shells were over or short of the target. They will then pass this information back to the battery by field telephone. (FSHM.)

High-explosive shells fired by the battery explode near the target. The battery is using indirect fire, meaning the target area is not visible from the gun positions. Based on the corrections received from the forward observer, the battery will recalculate the range and direction to the target for the next volley. This process continues until the shells hit the target. (FSHM.)

National Guard soldiers from 7th Illinois Infantry, mobilized for service on the Mexican border, practice digging trenches under the watchful eye of a regular Army training officer. The officer standing at left with his hands in his pockets is 2nd Lt. Dwight Eisenhower, 19th Infantry, future president of the United States. (FSHM.)

Two

The Leon Springs Military Reservation

During the First World War, the activity at the Leon Springs Military Reservation was concentrated in two areas. At the tent camp named Camp Bullis, troops from Camp Travis and Fort Sam Houston conducted weapons firing and maneuvering. In the western part of the reservation was Camp Stanley. Here, a cluster of specialized training camps and a remount station were set up. There was the First Officers Training Camp (FOTC) to develop officers for the 90th Division, mobilizing at Camp Travis. The training regimen would turn college-educated men into lieutenants in three months, hence the term "90-day wonders." These men began training in May 1917 and trained in the blazing Texas heat through June, July, and part of August. One of them, Phillip Lingle, chanted to himself as he trudged along the hot dusty trails, "The bear jumped over the Panther Bluff, Hell's Fire and Fuzzie-O!" His entire company quickly picked up the chant. The First Campers, as they were called, learned all the basic soldier skills—marksmanship, field fortifications, and small unit tactics—as well as leadership. Their motto was "Brave men shall not die because I faltered." The First Campers graduated on August 15.

Camp Samuel F.B. Morse trained signal battalion personnel. There were also camps for artillery and trench mortar units, cavalry, and field officers. When it became evident that cavalry was not in demand on the western front, cavalry units converted into field artillery units. The remount station received and trained horses for issue to all types of units.

Unlike Camp Bullis, which was almost exclusively composed of tents, Camp Stanley had quite a few mobilization buildings, similar to those at Camp Travis. After the war, the ammunition storage and processing functions of the San Antonio Arsenal were transferred to Camp Stanley. Someone figured out it was not a good idea to store tons of explosives in the city limits. The explosives were moved to Camp Stanley and stored in the temporary buildings. After the war, facilities at Camp Bullis were improved to support the billeting and training of troops during their periodic stints at the camp.

The view from Second Division Hill to the southeast shows some of the development of the camp since 1910. Though the five established campsites included some 70 buildings, tents were still the predominant form of shelter. The water tanks seen in the center of the photograph were added when the Army drilled wells to supply sufficient water for 10,000 troops. (FSHM.)

Soldiers in training line up in one of the tent camps at the Leon Springs Military Reservation as they prepare to go to the nearby rifle ranges. Based upon the uniform and equipment that these troops are wearing, this photograph would have been taken some time between 1910 and 1917. (FSHM.)

In 1917, the Army erected a headquarters building, seen here in the foreground, for the tent camp on the leased portion of the military reservation. The 90th Division named the tent camp Camp Bullis. Later, the name was applied to the entire military reservation, less the part occupied by Camp Stanley. (FSHM.)

Members of a band pose at the tent camp at the Leon Springs Military Reservation. In addition to playing music for parades and reviews, the band often played for the entertainment of the troops. In battle, members of the band would serve as litter bearers or provide security for the unit headquarters. (FSHM.)

In the northwest part of the reservation was the First Officer Training Camp, originally called Camp Funston. The State of Kansas wanted to name its cantonment after native son Frederick Funston, so the War Department renamed the cantonment for the FOTC Camp Stanley. Later, the area occupied by the several cantonments in that corner of the reservation was called Camp Stanley. (FSHM.)

It is laundry day for the First Campers at Camp Funston. The men used the sinks in the latrines behind their barracks to do their wash and hung the items out to dry. Within the camp, there were companies for cavalry, infantry, field artillery, engineers, and the air service. Upon graduation and commissioning, the men in each company would serve together in the same unit as lieutenants. (FSHM.)

Two First Campers spar with their bayonets. The man on the left has just parried, or blocked, the other man's thrust. Typically, fencing with bayonets during training was done with the scabbards on the bayonets in the interest of safety. The bayonets on these M1903 rifles have blades 16 inches long. (FSHM.)

Officer candidates at the First Officer Training Camp at Leon Springs attend church services. Many of these men came from the leading families in San Antonio. The First Campers included three future governors—Beauford Jester of Texas, James Beverly of Puerto Rico, and Charles Martin of Oregon—and future congressman Maury Maverick. (FSHM.)

Trenches (left) were a fact of life in the American Expeditionary Force. The troops learned the mechanics of constructing trenches and fortified emplacements as well as the tactics of siting them to optimize their fields of fire, cover, and concealment. Digging trenches during the hot Texas summer (below) also served as a conditioning and toughening exercise for the troops. Overseas, pioneer infantry regiments would often be assigned at the corps and field army levels to assist divisions with constructing and maintaining their entrenchments and performing other basic engineer tasks. This relieved the infantry of some of the labor involved in such tasks. (Both, FSHM.)

First Campers, above, pause from their spadework. This entrenchment appears to be a communications trench, as there are no embrasures to enable its occupants to fire their weapons while in it. A communications trench allowed troops to move between trench lines while under cover. It was also used to bring up supplies or evacuate casualties. At right, soldiers stand ready in a trench near Camp Stanley. The sides of the trench are revetted with planks to prevent the walls of the trench from caving in. Note the length of the bayonets. It was necessary to adapt the techniques of bayonet fighting to compensate for the unwieldiness of the bayonet in such close quarters. (Both, FSHM.)

Brig. Gen. David S. Stanley, for whom the camp was named, received the Medal of Honor for his Civil War heroism and served as the commander of the Department of Texas from 1884 to 1892. It was his recommendation that "a good range is essential" that led to the creation of the Leon Springs Military Reservation. (FSHM.)

First Campers take to the rifle range near the Schasse Ranch. As there are more firers than firing points, the non-firers are coaching the firers, marking the targets, and receiving other forms of training, such as the use of signal flags. In the background, the FOTC barracks are visible. (FSHM.)

Barbed-wire entanglements were another fact of life on the western front. In defense, they channelized the enemy into killing zones. In an attack, they were an obstacle to overcome so the attackers could close with the enemy. Troops learned how to set up and maintain them as well as how to breach them. (FSHM.)

Temporary barracks like these at Camp Stanley were built from standardized plans developed by the Quartermaster Department and published in *The Quartermaster's Handbook* in 1916. These buildings were austere and built with a minimum of skilled labor. They could accommodate any mobilization activity or be adapted for multiple purposes. (FSHM.)

At Camp Samuel F.B. Morse, signalmen practice installing telephone lines. Note the climbing belt on the soldier on the right. Stringing the lines along the tops of poles protected them from breaking by vehicles driving over them. Closer to the front, the lines were buried to protect them from shellfire. (FSHM.)

With their field gun limbered up, this M1917 gun section stands by at Camp Stanley. This field gun was of British design and American manufacture. This postcard is an example of clever marketing. Though it is titled as being at Camp Travis, the trees and buildings are unlike those at that camp. In fact, this image could be used to illustrate almost any mobilization cantonment. (FSHM.)

At the end of World War I, facilities at Camp Bullis were still primitive. These are the tents of Company K, 1st Infantry. The 1st Infantry was new to the 2nd Division. During the war, the 2nd Division included a marine brigade. When the Marine Corps returned to Navy control after the war, the 1st and 20th Infantry Regiments replaced the marines. (FSHM.)

Two cavalry officers, identified by their boots, watch a machine gun crew in action. As the gunner fires, the officer to his left observes the fall of shot with his binoculars. The gun is a .30-caliber Browning M1918 water-cooled machine gun. The second officer, leaning against the tree, watches the proceedings. (FSHM.)

Troops from the 9th Infantry Regiment hike to Camp Bullis. These soldiers are carrying their haversacks, gas masks, and individual weapons. Note the small number of men carrying rifles. This unit is probably one of the heavy-weapons companies armed with machine guns and mortars. Mule-drawn carts transport these weapons at the rear of the column. (FSHM.)

Cannoneers from the 2nd Division conduct service practice at Camp Bullis with the French-made M1897 field gun, the famous "French 75." These 75-millimeter guns were provided by France to the American Expeditionary Force during the First World War. These guns were known for their mobility and high rate of fire. (FSHM.)

American-made M1917 light tanks go to the range for target practice. Based on the French Renault FT light tank, the American version of this tank carried either a 37-millimeter cannon or a .30-caliber machine gun. These have the 37-millimeter gun. Above, the four tanks are seen from the flank. Below is the view from behind the firing line toward the targets. When not in use, the tanks stayed at Camp Bullis to save them from the wear and tear of the 40-mile trip from Fort Sam Houston to Camp Bullis and back. When the M2A2 light tank replaced the M1917 in 1937, some of the M1917s were retained for use as tractors. (Both, FSHM.)

The Schasse ranch house served as family quarters. In 1920, for example, it was home for Capt. Harvey Edward, 4th Field Artillery. The 4th Field Artillery, stationed at Camp Stanley from 1919 to 1922, was a pack artillery outfit; its cannons were disassembled and carried on pack mules for movement. (FSHM.)

The Scheele ranch house was built some time between 1888 and 1898 for Otto Scheele's family. It was used as quarters for the caretaker at Camp Bullis from 1921 to at least 1928. Enlarged in 1936, it was assigned to the commanding officer. More recently, the building was turned into office space for the natural and cultural resource managers who implement the Integrated Training Area Management Program. (FSHM.)

A couple of enterprising lieutenants connived to build this house with troop labor and locally available stone. The house was on the hillside overlooking the tent camp. When the house was finished and the lieutenants were ready to move in, a general officer ranked them out of it. (FSHM.)

The simple expedient of building a dam across a stream that flowed through the camp added a swimming pool to the cantonment. Local folklore has it that the pool was built by German prisoners of war. The POWs may have made some refinements during World War II, but by then, the pool was more than a decade old. (FSHM.)

Another addition to Camp Bullis in 1930 was an open-air theater. Besides permitting the showing of films or other entertainment, this building was also used as an auditorium or classroom for the training of troops. Later, it would be enclosed, allowing it to be used in any weather. (FSHM.)

This observation tower at one of the rifle ranges was built in 1933. From the upper deck, officers could observe the firing and enforce safety regulations. Field telephones would connect the tower to the target pits. A latrine and a storage room for targets and other range supplies were on the bottom level. (FSHM.)

This row of mess halls was built in the cantonment area along Wilkeson Road in 1930. Each mess hall had a full kitchen and a dining room, serving two rows of squad tents that housed a company of troops. These mess halls served the troops, Citizens Military Training Camp, Reserve Officer Training Corps, and, during the Roosevelt administration, Civilian Conservation Corps enrollees. (FSHM.)

A "hostess house" was added in the cantonment area in 1931. This was a servicemen's club at which a soldier could purchase refreshments, read, play cards, or just relax. This club had an outdoor dance pavilion. The cantonment also had an officers' mess, a post exchange gas station, and a post exchange. (FSHM.)

These two photographs show a bombing exercise conducted by the 8th and 90th Attack Squadrons from the 3rd Attack Group at Fort Crockett on November 3, 1930. The target was an airfield near Davis Ridge, about two miles northeast of the cantonment area. Above, bombers attack two lines of "weary willies," obsolete or retired aircraft, lined up on the airfield. Below, the explosions engulf the airfield. Twin-engine Keystone bombers made a series of attacks. These photographs show the first two attacks, which delivered 17-pound fragmentation bombs from an altitude of 400 feet. Later attacks consisted of three planes dropping salvoes of 100-pound demolition bombs. (Both, FSHM.)

Three

A Cinematic Interlude

After the War to End All Wars, garrison life at Fort Sam Houston settled into a dull peacetime routine. Drill, spit and polish, road marches, and trips to the range filled a soldier's calendar. In the 1920s, the new motion-picture industry hit upon the idea of making action movies paying tribute to veterans. The War Department went along with the idea, thinking it would inspire enlistments and improve morale. The Army provided technical advice and the use of military equipment and soldiers as movie extras. This provided the troops a break from the peacetime routine. The first movie filmed in San Antonio was *The Big Parade*, using the 2nd Division and Camp Bullis. In 1925, Paramount filmed parts of *The Rough Riders* at Camp Bullis. About 1,000 cavalrymen from Fort Clark and Camp Marfa deployed to Camp Bullis to storm San Juan Hill. Since the terrain at Camp Bullis did not resemble that of Cuba, the production company emplaced palm trees and other plants typical of Cuba on the terrain. Later, the hill in north-central Camp Bullis where the charge up San Juan Hill was filmed was designated Palm Tree Hill.

In April 1926, the 2nd Division deployed to Camp Bullis for the filming of Paramount's *Wings*. Here again, Camp Bullis did not look like Lorraine in France, so the production company brought in Lombardy poplars and tied them to the telephone poles along Bullis Road. Troops from the 2nd Division provided the proverbial "cast of thousands," portraying the American, French, and German soldiers, while the Air Corps provided squadrons for the German and American aircraft and set up the two aerodromes that were portrayed in the film. The climactic scenes in this film feature the American offensive at the Battle of Saint-Mihiel. The battle scenes were filmed in the western part of the reservation, where authentic trenches and bunkers were constructed. Tanks and infantry stormed these positions, while aircraft battled overhead. Released in 1927, *Wings* became the first movie to receive the Academy Award for Best Picture.

Rather than the French village of Mervale, this was an elaborate movie set. As actress Clara Bow drives her ambulance through Mervale, German bombers attack the town, menacing Bow and the wounded soldiers in a field hospital. Bow and the wounded are saved when fighter pilots Buddy Rogers and Richard Arlen drive the bombers off. (FSHM.)

The damage to the church in Mervale reveals it as a movie set in this view through the front entrance. The structural framework is plainly visible but could not be seen during the filming. During the attack by the German Gotha bombers, one of the German bombs hit the church, toppling the steeple. (FSHM.)

Fort Sam Houston troops take a break from cinematic combat. These men are playing French *poilus*, or World War I soldiers. There are equipped with the French helmets, coats, and accoutrements. Men from the 2nd Division also portrayed German soldiers and American doughboys for the battle scenes. The Western Players Protective Association complained that the use of soldiers put actors out of work. (FSHM.)

American-made M1917 tanks like these four from the 2nd Tank Company were used during the filming. Based on the French Renault FT design, the American version weighed in at six tons and mounted a Marlin or Browning machine gun or a 37-millimeter cannon in the rotating turret. It was powered by a four-cylinder Buda HU engine rated at 42 horsepower. (FSHM.)

A group of soldiers waits for the cue to begin the action. At the right is the M1916 37-millimeter gun. This gun fired high-explosive shells to destroy machine gun nests. Fired from a tripod or wheeled carriage, it could fire 35 rounds per minute and had an effective range of 1,500 meters. (FSHM.)

Two motion picture cameras can be seen at the left filming 2nd Division soldiers in French uniforms firing a field gun beneath a camouflage net. In this case, the camouflage does not adequately conceal the gun from aerial observation. The exposed sandbag parapet and other gear out in the open would give this position away. (FSHM.)

This aerial view of the movie battleground on the land north of the Schasse Ranch presents an accurate depiction of the western front as a treeless landscape, cut by long, irregular lines of trenches. The surface of the ground has been turned into a veritable moonscape of shell craters. (FSHM.)

This 155-millimeter M1917 howitzer, manufactured by Schneider-Creusot, was the heaviest field artillery piece used by the American divisions in France. Shown here in the traveling configuration, the piece has its tube pushed out of battery. This improved its balance on the road and made it easier to move into position. In the background are two Mack Bulldog trucks. (FSHM.)

For the climactic battle scenes in the movie, the production company constructed a network of trenches with extensive barbed-wire entanglements. Considering the number of World War I veterans still in the 2nd Division, the trenches and entanglements had to be just like the real thing. Beyond this trench are a field gun and three M1917 tanks. (FSHM.)

A mounted soldier rides past the church in the middle of the Mervale movie set. This shot was taken before the battle scene when actress Clara Bow and her ambulance are bombed by the Germans, because in that scene, the church suffers a direct hit that topples the steeple. (FSHM.)

Military and civilian sightseers pay a visit to Mervale, the movie set portraying a village in Lorraine. The mounted group stands near the crucifix that marks the entrance to the village. Clara Bow, the "It Girl," would drive by the crucifix on her way into town. In the background is the church. (FSHM.)

As the infantry advances across the cinematic battlefield, a captain of the 23rd Infantry described the scene: "Through the swirl of dust and smoke that at times hides the troops on the ground, flight after flight of airplanes whirr overhead." Veterans who participated in these scenes said the only thing missing was red wine and French bread. (FSHM.)

This complex of bunkers and fortifications was the final objective of the attacking doughboys. In addition to the two horsemen on top of the hill, there are several women and children at the lower right exploring the position. At the end of the ground battle scenes in the film, the camera zooms in on a German casualty sprawled on the cross. (FSHM.)

An aerial photograph of the area near Schasse Ranch at Camp Stanley taken in November 1934 shows part of the terrain representing the Saint-Mihiel battlefield in the movie. Trenches can be clearly seen in the lower left and upper center of the image. This image gives an appreciation of the intelligence value of aerial reconnaissance. (FSHM.)

Infantry and tanks swarm over the battlefield as pursuit planes roar overhead. The absence of explosions and smoke probably means that this is a rehearsal rather than the filming of the battle scene. William Wellman, the movie's director, had a tower built overlooking the battlefield so he could direct the scene and initiate the explosions. (FSHM.)

A trio of Martin MB-2 bombers makes a low pass over the battlefield during the battle scenes while another bomber flies overhead. Introduced in 1920, the MB-2 was the first American-designed bomber to be mass-produced. Powered by two Liberty engines, it had a four-man crew and a top speed of 99 miles per hour. (FSHM.)

This cracked-up Curtiss P-1 Hawk with German markings was a stand-in for the German Fokker D-VII fighter. Most of the Curtiss P-1s used in the film were from Kelly Field and were flown by Army pilots. Thomas Morse MB-3 fighters were painted and marked to play the French SPADs. (FSHM.)

Another World War I epic filmed at Camp Bullis was King Vidor's *The Big Parade*. While the camera crews stand ready, two actors portraying Germans, probably soldiers from Fort Sam Houston, are being coached by a director. In this scene, the Germans are using an American M1918 water-cooled machine gun. (FSHM.)

Four

Preparing for the "Big War"

In the 1930s, the routine of the peacetime Army prevailed. The onset of the Great Depression curtailed military spending, so the Army had to make do with the weapons and equipment left over from the First World War. The troops at Fort Sam Houston marched to Camp Bullis for marksmanship training and small unit training. The 2nd Division supported the CMTC encampments, ROTC summer camps, and Nation Guard annual training. During the administration of President Roosevelt, the 2nd Division supported Civilian Conservation Corps activities at Camp Bullis. The reservation was enlarged by 4,543 acres to accommodate the division-size garrison of Fort Sam Houston. The Camp Bullis headquarters building became the headquarters for the entire reservation.

Occasionally, the 2nd Division participated in maneuvers, which were usually referred to as "war games." Because the 2nd Division was the only nearly complete division stationed at a single installation, it was selected by the War Department to test a new organization for the Army's divisions. Field testing of the Provisional Infantry Division began in 1937, examining a division based on three regiments instead of four. In the following year, the Third Army conducted war maneuvers at Camp Bullis, emphasizing the transition from war games. After these maneuvers, the Army adopted the "triangular division" organization.

Shortly after the outbreak of war in Europe in September 1939, the United States began to mobilize. Bringing the Army and National Guard up to war strength meant more soldiers to train. This required another expansion of the training area at Camp Bullis. In 1941, about 8,700 acres were added to the reservation. Another 7,000 acres north of Cibolo Creek were leased as a maneuver area. With a large number of units and individuals being mobilized and organized at Fort Sam Houston, Camp Bullis served primarily for weapons firing. Unit maneuvering was conducted in the Louisiana Maneuver Area and to a limited extent in the leased area.

A battery of M1917 Schneider howitzers drives along a trail at Camp Bullis. These guns, first motorized in World War I due to a shortage of horses, were dropped from the 2nd Division after the war but restored in 1929. Their solid tire, wooden-spoke wheels limited their mobility. (FSHM.)

Through most of the 1930s, the infantry, like this column from the 9th Infantry heading home from Camp Bullis, moved by foot and mule. In the late 1930s, the field artillery was motorized. The gradual infusion of motor vehicles throughout the division helped realize the mobility demonstrated in the 1937 Provisional Infantry Test. (FSHM.)

Troops of the 2nd Division marching along Fredericksburg Road to Camp Bullis arrive at Nine-Mile Hill, the traditional stopping point along the way since at least 1911. The hill was called Nine-Mile Hill because it was nine miles from the post. Above, Company A, 9th Infantry, forms up and dresses its formation at close interval as other units march onto the campsite. Below, the troops set up a bivouac for an overnight stay before continuing to Camp Bullis for field training. The troops sleep two men to each pup tent. In this scene, they are lining up for chow served from the tent flies. (Both, FSHM.)

Two soldiers sit on their Indian motorcycles at Camp Bullis. This motorcycle was powered by a 45-cubic-inch V-twin engine and had a three-speed transmission. Some of the motorcycles shown here are equipped with a sidecar for a passenger. Motorcycles were used by messengers and reconnaissance units and for traffic control. (FSHM.)

A total of six bombproofs or concrete bunkers similar to this one were built on McCaskey Ridge, Neutze Hill, Light Hill, and Buck Hill. When these bunkers were used as artillery observation posts, field artillery and mortar forward observers could call for and adjust artillery fire onto targets close to the bunker in relative safety. (FSHM.)

A pair of sidecar motorcycles leads a convoy along Cowgill Road through the Cowgill Cut. This road led across Camp Bullis from Blanco Road along the eastern border of the reservation to the Schasse Ranch. The cut was made to reduce the steepness of the grade of this section of the road. (FSHM.)

At the 1935 session of the CMTC at Camp Bullis, Capt. W.S. Guy stands in front of Company C in the cantonment area. Each company was commanded by an active-duty officer assisted by a small cadre of Army Reserve officers and regular Army noncommissioned officers. CMTC had been conducted at Camp Bullis since 1924. (FSHM.)

CAMP BULLIS

The four photographs on these two pages show the Camp Bullis cantonment in the late 1930s with all the artillery and infantry of the 2nd Division in residence. Above, the delivery truck is driving southeast on Military Highway. To its right beyond the flagpole is the headquarters building used by the 2nd Division. Note that this building is seen in both photographs on the facing page. To the truck's left is the row of mess halls. The view below looks northwest and shows the area occupied by the artillery. The pool, restaurant, and barbershop separate the infantry and artillery tent areas. (Both, FSHM.)

Above is a view of the cantonment towards the southeast, looking up Military Highway. Across the bottom of the photograph is Bullis Road. At the left, above the long warehouse, is the 15th Field Artillery tent area. Farther left is the 12th Field Artillery area. The pool separates the 15th Field Artillery from the 23rd Infantry. Below, Military Highway runs past the headquarters building in the lower right. Officer tents would be set up between the highway and the row of mess halls. The open area beyond the tents doubled as a parade ground and landing strip. The pool and the field artillery tent areas are just to the left of the area shown in this photograph. (Both, FSHM.)

The kitchen crew of Battery B, 12th Field Artillery, poses at its kitchen in the cantonment area of Camp Bullis. In the left foreground is the stove section of the rolling kitchen, referred to as the "slum gun." Slum was short for slumgullion, a common meat and vegetable stew in the Army cook's manual. (FSHM.)

Demonstrating proper field hygiene, these troops from the 15th Field Artillery clean their mess kits. After washing the mess kits in hot, soapy water, the soldiers rinsed them in hot water. The final step was immersing them in boiling water to sterilize the mess kits. This process reduced the incidence of dysentery. (FSHM.)

An M2A2 light tank from the 2nd Tank Company crests a small rise in the ground during maneuvers. Tactically, this would expose the thinner armor on the underside of the tank to antitank gunfire. The M2A2, armed with machine guns, had an infantry support role and was not intended to fight other tanks. (FSHM.)

Elements of the 12th Cavalry Regiment, from the 1st Cavalry Division, arrive at Camp Bullis from Fort Brown, Texas, to take part in the Proposed Infantry Division Test. The column consists of M2 armored cars and cargo trucks. In this test, the cavalry would provide a highly mobile reconnaissance element. (FSHM.)

Companies of the 9th Infantry Regiment go to the known distance range at Camp Bullis. Above, the soldiers on the firing line are shooting the M1903 Springfield rifle from the sitting and offhand, or standing, positions. They will fire a specific number of rounds at bull's-eye targets at each of the specified distances, hence the name "known distance range." Below, the scorekeepers sit behind the firing line. The soldier in denim fatigues signals the pit crew to raise and lower the targets at each stage of the exercise. He talks on an EE-8 field telephone, introduced in 1932. On a good day, this battery-powered phone could transmit voice traffic 11 miles. (Both, FSHM.)

Above, the staff sergeant seated in the chair posts the scores of the firers on the easel. Two soldiers wear shooting coats, usually worn for competitive shooting. The currency pinned to the easel probably indicates bets were placed on the firers. Below, an important feature on this range was the mechanisms in the pit to raise and lower the targets. The firers engaged the targets while they were raised. The pit crew would then lower the targets, mark the hits, and raise the targets. The firers could then adjust their sights to correct their aim. Marksmanship was important, so the Army rewarded proficiency by adding a few dollars to a soldier's pay. For a soldier making $21 per month, every additional dollar equaled an almost five percent pay raise. (FSHM.)

During the Third Army Maneuvers in 1938, Lt. Gen. Herbert Brees stands before a map of the Leon Springs maneuver area and addresses the leaders of the units participating in the maneuvers. Seated on the platform are the generals of these units. This review and critique was essential to absorb the lessons learned. (FSHM.)

During the Proposed Infantry Division Maneuvers, a noncommissioned officer from the 9th Infantry Regiment signals to the rear. The soldier at the far right carries the M1918A1 Browning Automatic Rifle with the bipod mounted on the gas cylinder rather than near the muzzle as on later models. The others carry the M1903 Springfield rifle. (FSHM.)

The 2nd Division puts on a demonstration of some of the Army's latest equipment for CMTC students attending the July 1937 session at Camp Bullis. On display are a 75-millimeter pack howitzer used in the cavalry division and a 75-millimeter field gun. Beyond the guns is an M2A2 light tank. (FSHM.)

During the Third Army War Maneuvers, soldiers ham it up for the camera. While the soldiers take up positions behind the rocks and in the trees, the officer on top of the pole peers with his binoculars. The other officer looks at the map, ignoring what the sergeant is pointing at. (FSHM.)

From a hilltop at Camp Bullis, senior officers observe the Proposed Infantry Division Maneuvers. From left to right are two unidentified officers; Maj. Gen. James K. Parsons, 2nd Division commander; Maj. Gen. Herbert Brees, VIII Corps area commander; Brig. Gen. Leslie J. McNair, 2nd Division artillery commander; and Brig. Gen. Joseph W. "Vinegar Joe" Stilwell, 3rd Infantry Brigade commander. (FSHM.)

Capt. Verne D. Mudge and Pancho came to Camp Bullis with the 1st Reconnaissance Squadron, 1st Cavalry Division, for the Provisional Infantry Division Test. Captain Mudge would later serve as chief of staff of the 1st Cavalry Division and command its 2nd Brigade. During the Second World War, he commanded that division in the Southwest Pacific from 1943 to 1944. (FSHM.)

A group of cavalry and artillery officers confers over a map during the Proposed Infantry Division Test in 1937. The purpose of this test, conducted by a reinforced 2nd Division, was to evaluate a new divisional organization designed to increase the mobility of the division. In 1939, further tests at Camp Bullis led to the adoption of the "triangular division." (FSHM.)

During the Proposed Infantry Division Maneuvers in 1937, medics transport a simulated casualty on a wheeled litter. The wheeled litter allows only two litter bearers to move a casualty instead of the usual four. Note that the simulated casualty is still wearing all his equipment and carrying his rifle. (FSHM.)

A platoon of four M2A2 light tanks advances during the Proposed Infantry Division Test in 1937. The Rock Island Arsenal manufactured these 12-ton armored vehicles in 1935. They mounted two .30-caliber Browning air-cooled machine guns in their two side-by-side turrets. This feature earned the M2A2 the nickname "Mae West." (FSHM.)

An antitank gun takes up a firing position on the side of the road to engage a pair of "enemy" tanks. The antitank gun is an M1916 37-millimeter gun. The tanks are M2A2 light tanks. Gun flashes on the gun and the tank were added during the processing of the film. (FSHM.)

During the Provisional Infantry Division Maneuvers in 1937, a battery of 37-millimeter antitank guns engages a pair of M2A2 light tanks as they approach its position. An officer directs the battery from his position to the right rear of his three guns. The gun on the left has just fired. (FSHM.)

A battalion of the 141st Infantry Regiment of the 36th Division, Texas National Guard, marches along Wilkeson Road in the cantonment area on the way to the parade ground for a review. The reviewing party will include the division's commanding general, Claude V. Birkhead. These troops carry the M1903 Springfield rifle. (FSHM.)

The 141st Infantry Regiment Band, led by WO Otto Zoeller, parades through the cantonment in August 1938 during the Third Army War Maneuvers. The band was part of the 36th Division, Texas National Guard. The 36th Division was part of the Blue Forces fighting the 2nd and 45th Divisions of the Brown Forces. (FSHM.)

Maj. Gen. Claude V. Birkhead, commander of the 36th Division, salutes as he reviews his troops at Camp Bullis on August 10, 1938. To the right of Birkhead is Gov. W. Lee O'Daniel of Texas. Second to the right of O'Daniel is his successor as governor of Texas, James V. Allred. (FSHM.)

On the road leading to Camp Bullis, a construction crew builds a pair of limestone block columns in 1939. The main entrances at Fort Sam Houston had been marked with similar columns reminiscent of Fort Sam Houston Quadrangle, the 1976 depot building occupied by the Eighth Corps Area headquarters. (FSHM.)

From this building, constructed in 1917 as the headquarters of Camp Bullis, the Camp Bullis Detachment managed the ranges and maneuver areas. Used temporarily for quartermaster activities after the First World War, it was renovated in 1937 and converted back to the camp headquarters. Readers can compare this view with the images on pages 23 and 126. (FSHM.)

A battalion of the 2nd Engineers from Fort Logan, Colorado, arrives at Camp Bullis to participate in maneuvers evaluating the "triangular division" concept. The engineers would be part of a streamlined mechanized force. Their mission was to facilitate the division's movement on the offensive by clearing obstacles and to reinforce the division's defense by building obstacles and field fortifications. (FSHM.)

Two officers from the 12th Field Artillery check each other for ticks. The lone star tick, or *Amblyomma americanum*, could transmit a febrile disease known as Bullis fever. Late in World War II, the Army curtailed large-scale training at Camp Bullis due to these ticks. A massive eradication campaign after the war reduced the tick problem to a mere nuisance. (FSHM.)

On August 8, 1940, elements of the 38th Infantry arrive at Camp Bullis on Wilkeson Road. This unit had recently been assigned to the 2nd Division as part of the "triangular division" reorganization. These troops are riding in T202-series Dodge reconnaissance cars. They would soon deploy to Louisiana for maneuvers. (FSHM.)

A machine-gunner takes aim with an M1918A1 Browning machine gun on the range. The gunner wears the older blue denim fatigues that were used occasionally as a field uniform. The sergeant at left wears the olive drab herringbone twill fatigue uniform introduced in 1941. Both are wearing the "Daisy Mae" hat, like that worn by the Al Capp cartoon character of the same name. (FSHM.)

At a headquarters in a field location during the Third Army 1941 maneuvers, a warrant officer talks on a field telephone. The soldier behind the typewriter wears coveralls and a field cap, indicating that this is probably a maintenance unit. Though the Army standardized the M1 helmet in 1941, this unit still wears the M1921 helmet. (FSHM.)

Soldiers from the 2nd Division fire the M1 rifle and the M1918 Browning Automatic Rifle, or BAR, on the known distance range. The M1 firers are on the left; the BAR firers are on the right. The soldier to the right of each BAR firer acts as coach and assistant gunner. (FSHM.)

A technical sergeant, staff sergeant, two corporals, and a technician, fifth grade, are part of the 68-man Camp Bullis Detachment, which operated Camp Bullis during the Second World War. This detachment, part of the 1857th Army Service Unit, which ran Fort Sam Houston, included a headquarters element, a quartermaster section, and a signal section. (FSHM.)

These three soldiers illustrate the transition of uniforms in the early days of the war. The soldier in the center wears the old blue denim fatigues. On the left is a cotton coverall, intended for tank crews and vehicle mechanics. On the right is the new herringbone twill uniform. All three wear the M1 steel helmet. (FSHM.)

This range at Camp Bullis can handle 40 firers at a time. With a firer and a coach at each firing point and two men in the target pits for each target, every man in an infantry company armed with a rifle could be qualified by rotating through each of the four positions. (FSHM.)

A military police officer stands with two ladies at the new camp chapel on the day it opened in 1945. No longer would the soldiers have to attend religious services in a tent or mess hall. The officer is wearing the service uniform, referred to as "pinks and greens," even though the trousers were officially "drab, light shade." (FSHM.)

Five

A New Mission

When the Second World War ended, Fort Sam Houston and Camp Bullis had reached a dead end as far as having a modern combat division as their garrison. Though the post had ample billeting space for more than the division's 20,000 troops, its sub-post Camp Bullis, with 29,000 acres of land, was too small to safely accommodate tank gunnery, and the flight paths in and out of the San Antonio Municipal Airport restricted artillery and mortar firing. Rather than assign a division to garrison Fort Sam Houston, the War Department decided to develop the post as the major training site for the Army Medical Department, one of its largest branches. In 1945, the Army Medical Department already had a significant presence at Fort Sam Houston in the form of the Brooke Hospital Center, the largest medical facility in the Army, and the small Medical Service School. Since the Medical Field Service School at Carlisle Barracks, Pennsylvania, had outgrown its facilities there, it moved to Fort Sam Houston in 1947.

Lackland Air Force Base, previously part of Kelly Field, became the "gateway to the Air Force" in 1947 when the Air Force established its basic military training school there. The airmen would go to Camp Bullis for weapons qualification. The training of the Air Police at Lackland added to the Air Force presence at Camp Bullis. The cantonment area, training facilities, and firing ranges continued to be improved.

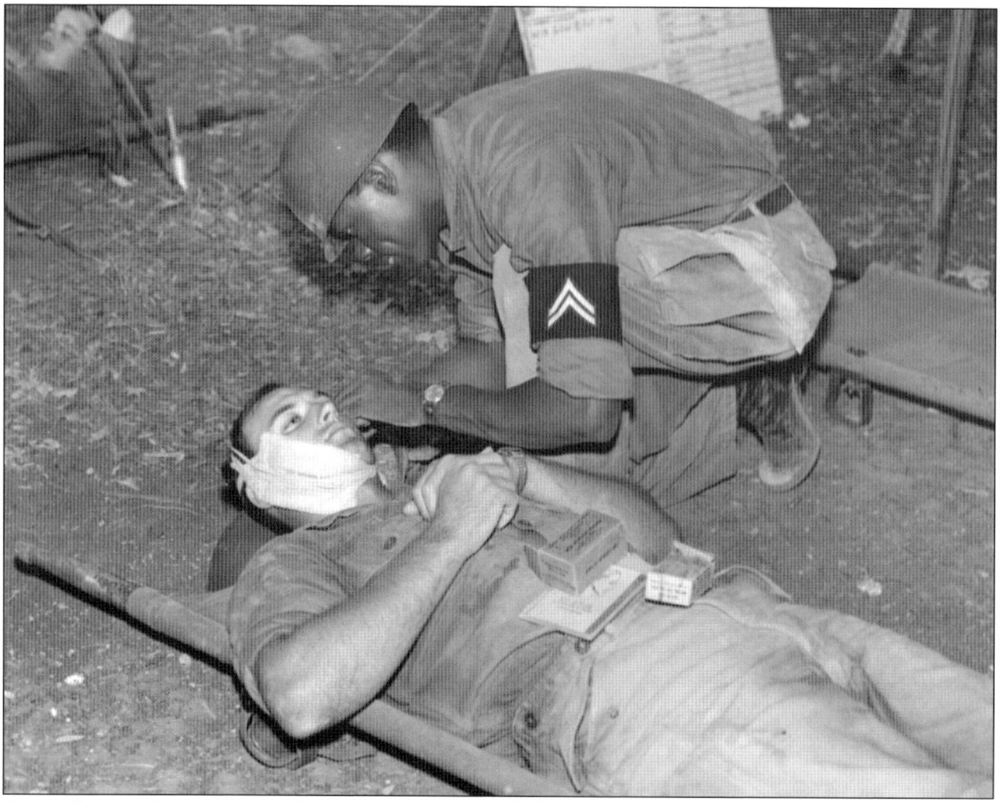

A combat medic trainee applies a face bandage on a classmate's simulated wound in a practical exercise in the medics' advanced individual training. Completion of this course of instruction will qualify the soldier in the military occupational specialty of medical aidman. Some of the trainees in this program are conscientious objectors. (FSHM.)

Combat medic trainees at the US Army Medical Training Center conduct a training exercise in the use of improvised litters. Here, the trainees use a blanket and tent poles to make a litter. Other techniques involve the use of shirts, jackets, or a poncho with tent poles or other improvised poles. (FSHM.)

A Piasecki H-25 helicopter, nicknamed the "Army Mule," hovers to deliver a box of medical equipment during a demonstration at Camp Bullis. This aircraft was a tandem rotor helicopter used by the Army as a light cargo and utility aircraft. With a crew of two, it could accommodate five passengers or two litter patients. (ACHH.)

Members of the 312th Logistics Command Engineer Section pause during a map exercise at their annual training at Camp Bullis in 1961. Behind these Army Reservists is the situation map, depicting the locations of the units portrayed in this exercise. A logistics command managed supply and services functions in the rear area of a combat zone. (FSHM.)

M.Sgt. George A. Hibdon, the noncommissioned officer in charge of the Fourth Army Communications Center at Camp Bullis, works at his desk, while Sp5c. Robert Logan Jr., the transmitter repairman, stands by. This system provided communication links for the Fourth Army Headquarters at Fort Sam Houston. (FSHM.)

A security police trainee chows down on a C-ration meal. There were several menus of rations within a case of 12 meals. Each contained a meat entrée, a dessert of canned fruit or crackers and candy, and a bread or cake item. Most of the entrées were palatable when heated. (USAFSFM.)

A staff sergeant takes aim with an M1 carbine. This lightweight weapon was the principal shoulder arm of the Air Police. In 1960, the Air Police School and the Air Force Marksmanship Unit tested the Armalite AR15 rifle at Camp Bullis. In 1965, the Air Force adopted the AR15 as the M16 to replace the carbine. (USAFSFM.)

During its second week of training at Camp Bullis in 1967, the 44th Evacuation Hospital established this 100-bed hospital. In a combat zone, an evacuation hospital would typically have a 400-bed capacity. It would receive all types of patients and be able to perform major medical and surgical treatments. (FSHM.)

Soldiers engage targets on the Trainfire Range with the M16A1 rifle. Instead of shooting at bull's-eye targets at known distances, the soldier must detect a pop-up silhouette target and engage it before it disappears. If the soldier hits the target, it falls and the soldier scores a point. This system, adopted in 1957, provided a more realistic method of training soldiers to shoot. (FSHM.)

A staff sergeant from the Medical Training Center demonstrates firing the M16 rifle on full automatic. He cants the rifle so the recoil will make the muzzle sweep across the target. The soldier at the left is the safety noncommissioned officer. Both men are combat veterans, indicated by the insignia on their right sleeves. (FSHM.)

These two views of a company street illustrate the relatively comfortable conditions that the troops experienced in the cantonment area. The tents were set up with wood frames on concrete slabs and had electric lights. Above is the view towards the mess hall with a kitchen and dining room that could double as a classroom. Below is the view in the opposite direction, towards the latrine. The latrine had hot and cold running water in the showers and sinks. It also provided urinal troughs and flush toilets. In 1969, hutments replaced the tents. These were wood-frame structures on concrete pads, about the same size as the tents. (Both, ACHH.)

In 1965, the Vietnam Village was created at Camp Bullis to give soldiers deploying to Vietnam experience of some of the situations they would meet in-country. The symbols on the sign are, from left to right, the Combat Infantry Badge, the insignia of the US Army Medical Training Center, and the Combat Medic Badge. (FSHM.)

Sfc. Kenneth Lewis, far right, without a helmet, begins the Republic of Vietnam Training Course with an in-depth orientation. This course was presented by the Military Science Branch of the US Army Medical Training Center to its students but also to individuals and units scheduled to deploy to Vietnam. (FSHM.)

At this training station, M.Sgt. Henry C. Morgan describes the types of mines and booby traps the soldiers might encounter in Vietnam. For the trainees' walk through the Vietnam Village, the instructors emplaced mines and booby traps to see whether the trainees detected them or fell victim to them. (FSHM.)

At the entrance to the Vietnam Village are the people who developed and organized it. Standing, from left to right, are S. Sgt Robert B. Schults in a Viet Cong uniform; Maj. Gen. William A. Harris, creator of the Vietnam Village; M. Sgt. Henry C. Morgan; and Capt. Marmon F. Cope. Kneeling are Sgt. W. T. Wilson, left, and S. Sgt Harvie T. Stanford. (FSHM.)

ROTC cadets head off into the brush on a reconnaissance patrol during their summer camp in June 1967. The cadets carry M1 rifles and wear olive green fatigue uniforms. As stealth is a prerequisite, the cadets have tied down their trousers legs to minimize noise as they move through the brush. (FSHM.)

Trainee medics from the Medical Training Center unload rifle racks and issue M16s. The absence of magazine pockets on their belts would indicate they are going to zero the weapons. The soldier at the right with the armband is an acting noncommissioned officer. Units rotate leadership positions among the trainees to give everyone leadership experience. (FSHM.)

During a tactical field training exercise in 1967, combat medic trainees at a field medical installation unload a simulated patient from an M43 ambulance. The M43 ambulance, commonly referred to as the "cracker box," can carry four litters or six ambulatory patients. The M43 was built by the Dodge Motor Company. (FSHM.)

In this training exercise, a unit practices triage, the system of sorting and prioritizing casualties. The goal is to provide the greatest good to the greatest number. Medical personnel are taught that the commitment of resources should be decided first based on the mission and immediate tactical situation and then by medical necessity. (FSHM.)

The 41st Surgical Hospital tested the MUST system at Camp Bullis in February 1969. Patient care areas are in the inflatable sections resembling Quonset huts. The operating rooms, laboratory, X-ray facility, and pharmacy are in the rectangular containers marked with a red cross. In the upper left is a helipad. (FSHM.)

A CH-47 Chinook helicopter delivers one of the containers for the MUST equipment to the 45th Surgical Hospital in August 1966. This is an expandable unit that opens into a 206-square-foot space. The equipment for the laboratory, pharmacy, X-ray, surgery, or dental facility would be contained in this type of unit. (FSHM.)

Two soldiers from the 25th Surgical Hospital ride the top of a MUST section as it inflates. The utility unit in the upper left not only inflates the units but also supplies heat, cooling, and electrical power. When completely inflated, this section will contain a 25-bed ward. This unit hails from St. Louis, Missouri. (ACHH.)

Soldiers from the 41st Combat Support Hospital work as a team inside an inflatable MUST section. The two soldiers at right are setting up the air-conditioning ducts. The soldiers in the background are installing the floor. When fully set up, this module will be part of a 100-bed-capacity hospital. (ACHH.)

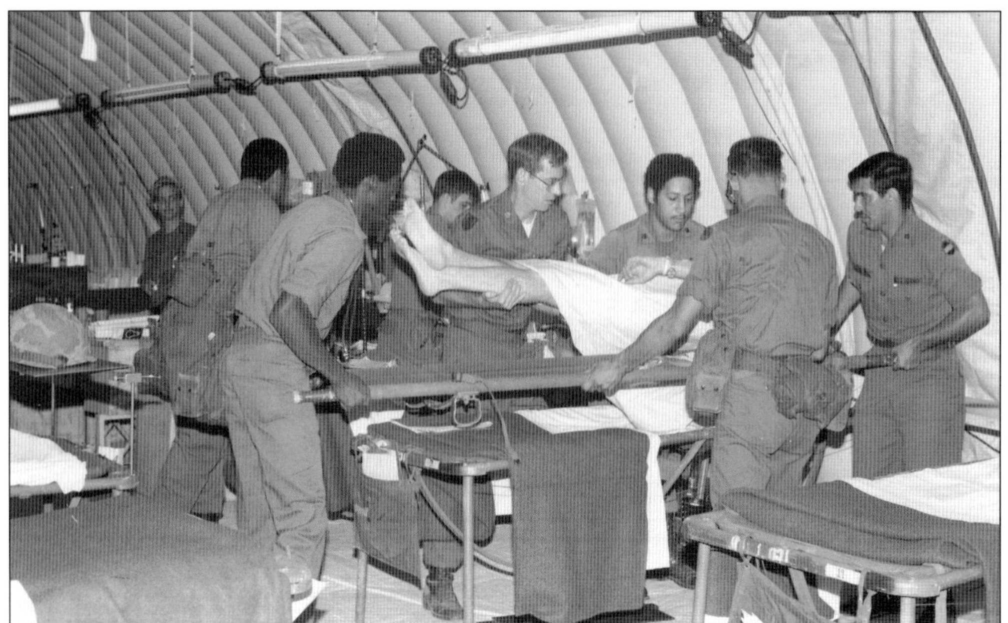

Medics in a MUST ward transfer a simulated patient from a bed to a litter. This exercise involved the 41st Combat Support Hospital, the 507th Medical Company, and the 485th Medical Detachment. They were joined by doctors and nurses from Brooke Army Medical Center in the Professional Filler System (PROFIS). In PROFIS, key specialists working in hospitals were designated to deploy with tactical medical units. (ACHH.)

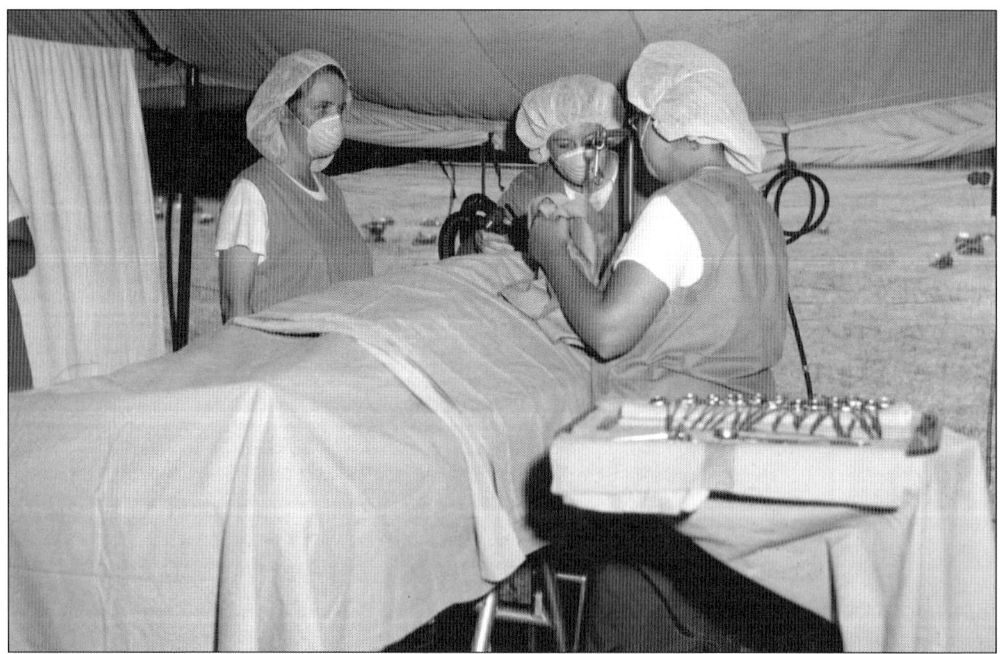

A doctor, a nurse, and an anesthetist prepare a simulated patient for surgery during an exercise at a field hospital at Camp Bullis for students at the Medical Field Service School Officer Basic Course. In the Officer Basic Course, the students learn to apply their medical skills in a tactical field environment. (ACHH.)

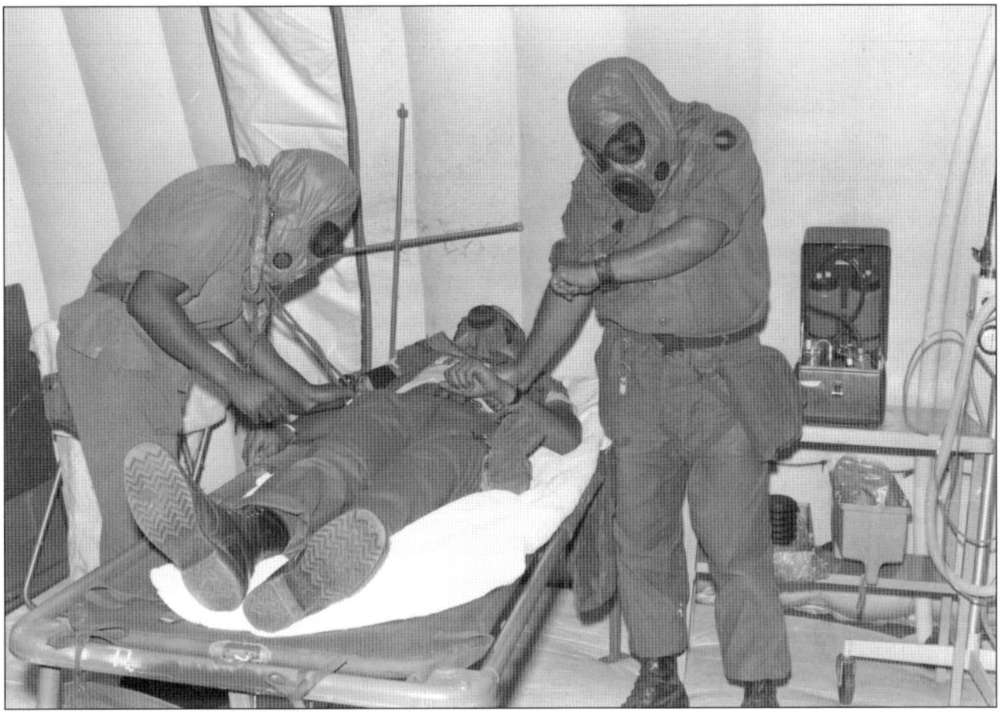

Medics from the 41st Combat Support Hospital assess a simulated casualty inside a MUST shelter. The medics and the casualty wear M17 protective masks to prevent inhaling chemical agents. Greater protection is afforded by donning the chemical protective suits lined with activated charcoal and the rubber boots and gloves. (FSHM.)

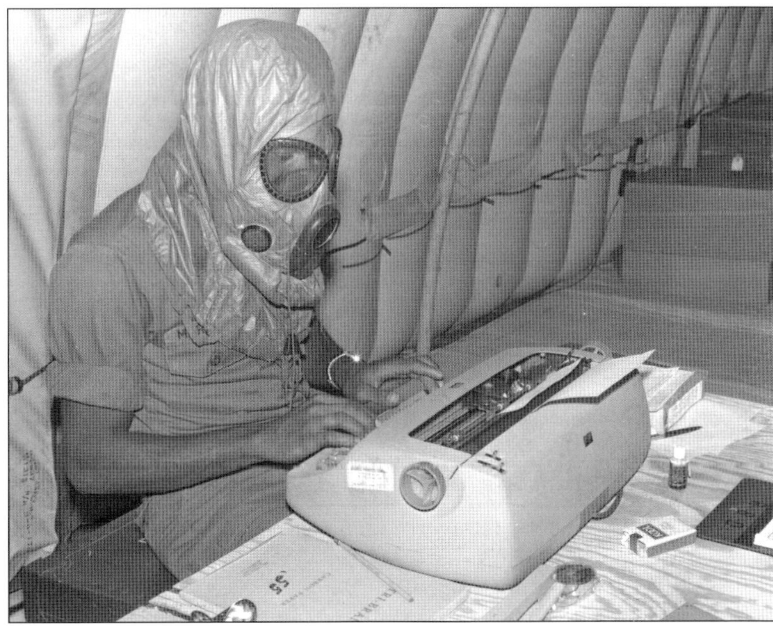

Not even a simulated chemical attack can keep Spc. Donald Marchant of the 41st Combat Support Hospital from completing his paperwork. After donning his M17 protective mask, he types away within an inflated MUST facility at Camp Bullis. A soldier must be able to put on and clear this mask within nine seconds. (FSHM.)

A colonel conducts a weapons familiarization for students from the Medical Field Service School. In the foreground are an M2 60-millimeter mortar and an M1 81-millimeter mortar. On the table are an M60 machine gun, an M14 rifle, an M79 grenade launcher, hand and rifle grenades, and a bayonet. Beyond the table are an M2 machine gun and a recoilless rifle. (ACHH.)

After finishing a combat casualty evacuation exercise, the trainees from the US Army Medical Training Center experience "concurrent training" while waiting for their classmates to finish the exercise. Rather than have trainees stand idle, the Army has them learn the contents of the field dispensary kit they will use. (FSHM.)

This aerial view of the Camp Bullis cantonment area shows, from left to right, Military Highway leading to the flagpole by the camp headquarters at the top of the image, the row of dining facilities along Wilkeson Road, the two hutment areas separated by the pool, and the parade ground. (ACHH.)

Black Jack Village supports the training of combat medics. It contains a bivouac area and an assembly area plus training stations for selected medical tasks. Located nearby is the litter obstacle course. The village was named for Col. Jack Wallace, who was commander of the Medical Training Center in 1972. (FSHM.)

Physicians from the armed services and the Public Health Service fire the M16 rifle. They are participating in a graduate-level program that prepares health care professionals for direct support of combat operations. This program, the Combat Casualty Care Course, was instituted by Lt. Gen. Charles Pixley, the Army surgeon general from 1977 to 1981. (ACHH.)

Maj. Gen. Spurgeon Neel, far left, commander of the Health Services Command, and Maj. Gen. Edward Vogel, center, superintendent of the Academy of Health Sciences, receive a briefing on a land navigation exercise for officers attending the Medical Corps, Dental Corps, and Veterinary Corps basic courses at the academy in 1976. (ACHH.)

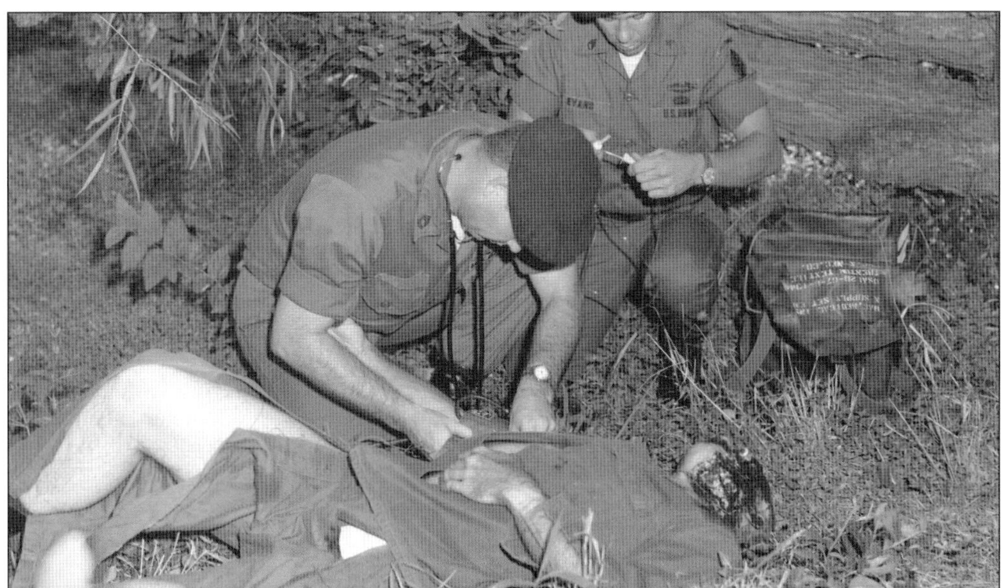

Special Forces medical sergeants treat simulated casualties at Camp Bullis. Above, the sergeant at right checks a casualty's pulse while the other soldier prepares an IV infusion. At right, the medical sergeant attaches a blood pressure cuff. In the Special Forces A Team, there are two medical sergeants, trained primarily in trauma medicine. They are also proficient in dentistry, veterinary medicine, public sanitation, water quality, and optometry. In addition to the two medical sergeants, other members of the A Team are cross-trained in trauma medicine. Special Forces medical sergeants and communications sergeants have been coming to Camp Bullis to train since 1952. (Both, ACHH.)

Col. Alvin O. Hall stands by the drop zone that bears his name. The drop zone, completed in 1980 during Hall's tenure as garrison commander at Fort Sam Houston, was built to support parachute and airmobile operations. Units of the 101st Airborne Division prepared the drop zone during an EDRE. (FSHM.)

The 1st Cavalry Division from Fort Hood, Texas, deployed a clearing station to Camp Bullis in 1981. Set up under camouflage nets, this clearing station included an operating room, a dental tent, and a surgical recovery ward. The easel and the large 1st Cavalry Division insignia indicate this was a demonstration rather than a tactical exercise. (ACHH.)

During an EDRE for units of the 82nd Airborne Division at Camp Bullis in 1980, paratroopers parachuted into Drop Zone Hall, located between Butte Hill and Pike Hill, following an air move from Fort Bragg, North Carolina. Above, some of the paratroopers are still in the air as others have landed and are "rolling up the stick," or assembling. Below, the paratroopers, clad in the lightweight camouflaged fatigues and jungle boots and armed with M16 rifles, are deploying to pursue and engage the enemy. In this operation, students from the Security Police Academy played the role of the enemy. (Both, USAFSFM.)

Two noncommissioned officers from the 307th Medical Battalion, part of the 82nd Airborne Division, wait under a camouflage net during a tactical problem involving a mass casualty exercise in 1980. The 307th would return to Camp Bullis in 1985 to conduct an airdrop with a French army medical unit. (ACHH.)

An instructor teaches a class on the use of the M2 lensatic compass in land navigation. Using a topographic map and a compass, the students will navigate cross-country through a series of points to reach a designated endpoint. These troops are wearing the woodland pattern camouflage battle dress uniform introduced in 1981. (ACHH.)

Even in a modern tactical environment where wheeled or tracked ambulances and helicopters are available to move casualties, the four-man litter team still plays a vital role. Litter teams can move casualties from areas where it is unsafe for vehicles and medical evacuation aircraft to operate. They will also transfer casualties between vehicles and medical facilities. At right, Spc. Sam Snider stands by to demonstrate the litter carry. Below, a team of trainees at the Medical Training Center moves a casualty on a litter. Note that they are crouching as they move, as they would in a combat situation. (Both, ACHH.)

One of the basic skills taught to the combat medic is mastery of litter drill. The litter obstacle course at Black Jack Village tests the medics' strength and ingenuity. Above, the litter team carries the casualty up a flight of stairs. The trick here is to keep the litter horizontal. The medics at the back must raise their end as the front pair ascends the steps. Below, the passage under a barbed wire obstacle is a test of strength. Each medic can use only one arm to overcome the weight of the casualty and the friction of the litter against the ground. (Both, ACHH.)

Passage of a litter team through a narrow space such as a footbridge, right, or a doorway is also a test of strength. Only two of the medics can support the litter at a time. Below, the litter team passes a wall obstacle. The front two support their end of the litter on the wall, then climb over it. They resume carrying their end and advance the litter so the wall supports the rear end of the litter. Then the rear pair of medics climbs over the wall and resumes carrying their end of the litter. (Both, ACHH.)

In 1985, the US Army Medical Equipment Board tested vertical rescue techniques at Camp Bullis. These techniques would facilitate the movement of casualties in mountain areas and across rivers. Graduates of the Combat Medical Specialist Course received a week of classroom instruction on the equipment and one week of mountaineering training. Above, the medics have prepared a litter patient for the single-rope bridge. Before sending the litter patient across, a member of the litter team must cross the bridge carrying a rope attached to the litter. Below, the litter and the patient are pulled across the Cibolo Creek. (Both, ACHH.)

Transfer of Air Police training to Lackland Air Force Base in 1956 added another customer for the ranges and training areas at Camp Bullis. The Air Police were renamed the Security Forces, recognizing the air base defense role. The Security Forces are one of the largest career fields within the Air Force. (USAFSFM.)

A staff sergeant maintains overwatch of the firing line with his M60 machine gun. This 23-pound gun, introduced in 1957, fires 550 rounds per minute from a disintegrating metallic link belt. One man can fire the gun from the shoulder or hip, as shown here. It can also be fired on the ground from its integral bipod or a tripod. (USAFSFM.)

A basic security specialist practices apprehending an intruder who is attempting to enter a restricted area at Victor Base. This training area was set up in 1977 near the Schasse Ranch for the Security Forces and includes a mock airfield. The aircraft in the background is an F-100 Super Saber. (USAFSFM.)

On November 30, 1970, the first six women graduated from the Security Police Academy. The group pictured here is the first all-female class to graduate. In 1976, the Air Force abolished the Women's Air Force Directorate, eliminating the final distinction between women and men. This was two years before the Army abolished the Women's Army Corps. (USAFSFM.)

A convoy transporting troops prepares to move out. M706 armored cars manned by the Security Forces provide the escort. The armored cars are spread through the length of the convoy to ensure that in the event of an ambush, some of them will be able to maneuver to engage the ambushers. (USAFSFM.)

An M706 armored car covers a group of dismounted Security Forces troops along the edge of the woods with its machine gun. The Air Force tested the M706 armored cars in 1962 and 1963 and used them for air base security in Vietnam, Korea, and the Southwest Asia theater of operations. (USAFSFM.)

A squad of security police deploys from the rear of an M113 armored personnel carrier and takes up firing positions. The M113, introduced in 1960, carried 11 passengers plus driver and vehicle commander. Armed with a machine gun, the M113 had armor that protected its crew from small arms fire and shell fragments. (USAFSFM.)

Sometimes it takes more than rifles and pistols to defend an air base. In that case, the Security Forces can deploy the .50-caliber M2 machine gun, affectionately known as "Ma Deuce." A technical sergeant and an airman conduct mechanical training with dummy ammunition, practicing the loading and clearing procedures for the gun. (USAFSFM.)

Even larger threats were engaged with the M72 Light Antitank Weapon, or LAW. The LAW fired a 66-millimeter-diameter rocket from a disposable launch tube. The high-explosive antitank warhead can penetrate 12 inches of armor at ranges out to 200 meters. Here, airmen conduct a dry-fire exercise with the expended launchers. (USAFSFM.)

A gunner takes aim with the M67 recoilless rifle. This 90-millimeter weapon gave the Security Forces a real anti-armor capability. Its high-explosive antitank ammunition could penetrate 10 inches of armor plate at a range of 300 meters. Operated by a crew of three, this recoilless rifle also fired an antipersonnel round. (USAFSFM.)

Marines (in camouflage uniforms) and airmen (in berets) chow down on C-rations. In 1982, the Marine Corps enrolled its military police personnel in Air Force Security Police Academy courses. Previously, they had trained with the Army. Navy and Coast Guard Shore Patrolmen had been enrolled with the Security Police Academy since 1973. (USAFSFM.)

A group of security police trainees prepares to move out on maneuvers. This end-of-course exercise gave students an opportunity to apply the combat skills they learned in the course. Starting in October 1999, this exercise, called Warrior Week, presented a realistic expeditionary experience in tactics, basic field hygiene, and survival skills. (USAFSFM.)

Six

Admirably Suited to All Purposes

In 1891, Brig. Gen. David S. Stanley stated the need for a maneuver area and firing range for Fort Sam Houston. It took 15 years to acquire a suitable tract of land. Since its initial purchase in 1906, the Leon Springs Military Reservation has grown in size and in the number and types of its facilities to support the changing training needs of the Army. The land acquired then and subsequently added to the reservation has proven to be very adaptable to those needs though the Army has changed from a foot- and horse-mobile force to a modern force equipped with motor vehicles and aircraft, armed with powerful individual and crew-served weapons, and using high-technology systems to support tactical operations, logistics, and administration.

In addition to being a training ground, Camp Bullis served as the proving ground for numerous technical and tactical innovations. These innovations included the M16 rifle; the Medical Unit, Self-contained, Transportable; the Deployable Medical System; and the triangular division, to name a few of the most important ones.

What began as a firing range and maneuver area for infantry, cavalry, and field artillery has become a training ground for the medical personnel of all the armed services and the Air Force Security Forces while still meeting most of the field training needs of the National Guard and Reserve units in the region. The varied nature of the terrain, the amount of land, the year-round good climate, and the easy access to Camp Bullis from local posts and bases have all contributed to its adaptability for a wide variety of uses. The ability of Camp Bullis and the Leon Springs Military Reservation to accommodate the changing needs of the Army over a period of more than a century confirms the wisdom of the initial selection of this piece of land as admirably suited to all types of military training and bodes well for the continued development and use of Camp Bullis for many years to come.

Like the doughboys almost six decades before him, this airman at the Air Police Academy digs in at Camp Bullis. He is wearing the All-purpose, Lightweight, Individual Carrying Equipment, or ALICE, introduced in 1974. With this system, he can attach a variable load of accessories to his nylon belt and suspenders, depending on his mission requirements. (USAFSFM.)

A camouflaged Air Force C-130 Hercules cargo aircraft takes off from the Combat Assault Landing Strip, or CALS, near the northern boundary of Camp Bullis. The compressed-gravel 3,600-foot-long runway permits the delivery or pickup of personnel, vehicles, or cargo during field exercises. Parking areas adjacent to the runway can accommodate seven aircraft. (FSHM.)

Reserve component soldiers apply camouflage while preparing for a patrol. In addition to their load-bearing equipment, they are wearing the Multiple Integrated Laser System, or MILES, on their weapons, helmets, and torsos. This system, similar to laser tag, adds realism to tactical training by emphasizing the use of cover and marksmanship. (FSHM.)

A machine gun crew from the 288th Service Company engages targets on the 10-meter range with an M60 machine gun. Here, it fires at silhouette targets that at 10 meters appear as large as man-size targets at normal battlefield ranges. Next, the crew moves to the Trainfire Range, where targets pop up randomly at various ranges for the crew to engage. (FSHM.)

Security police trainees receive a briefing at the Base Defense Operations Center, or BDOC, before beginning a tactical exercise. The BDOC is the command post for the Security Forces defending an air base. The defenders will be subjected to a series of realistic situations they might experience in the real world. (USAFSFM.)

On the perimeter of a simulated air base during a practical exercise, the security police trainees run the checkpoint at the entrance to the base. They will examine the credentials of anyone trying to enter the base. The enemy may try to enter by force or stratagem. It is up to the trainees to keep them out. (USAFSFM.)

Future combat medics, dressed in the woodland pattern battle dress uniforms, negotiate the "high step" event on the obstacle course. Each trainee must step over a series of logs placed just below waist level while keeping his hands clasped behind his head. Obstacle courses require strength and agility while building the soldier's confidence. (FSHM.)

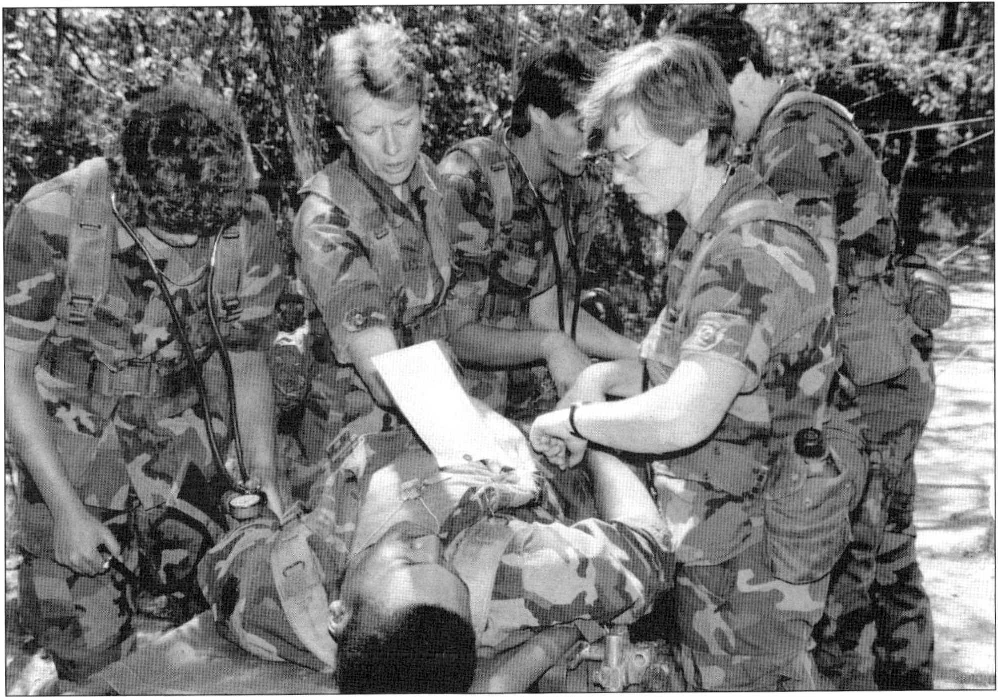

An all-female team of physicians and medical specialists examines a simulated casualty at a nuclear, biological, and chemical battalion aid station. At this type of aid station, the casualties would be decontaminated prior to being treated. These soldiers are Army Reservists of the 323rd Medical Laboratory from Boston, Massachusetts. (ACHH.)

The Deployable Medical System (DEPMEDS) began to replace the MUST in 1988. The DEPMEDS is a collection of air-transportable standardized modules that can be assembled to meet a specific mission. Modules include a laboratory, radiology, a pharmacy, a sterilization section, and an operating room in rigid shelters. Other functions are contained in expandable modular tents. (FSHM.)

At Camp Bullis, the Deployable Medical System Equipment for Training, or DEMSET, shown in this aerial view, is designed to train Army medical units that are issued the DEPMEDS. A complete set of the equipment is in place there, allowing units to train on the equipment without having to transport it from their home stations. (FSHM.)

Spc. David Dorfman races against the clock while assembling an M9 and M16 after donning a protective mask as part of the 2016 Army Contracting Command Best Warrior Competition. The competition consisted of a series of events over four days testing the mental and physical agility of 10 soldiers. Dorfman is assigned to the 389th Army Band at Redstone Arsenal, Alabama. (DVIDS.)

Airmen enrolled in the Security Forces Academy advance cautiously toward a simulated ambush point during a training mission at the Combat Leadership Course. Two of these airmen are armed with the M203 grenade launcher. The course focuses on leadership, teamwork, and tactics while performing security operations in a combat environment. (DVIDS.)

Spc. Austin Hunsaker (bottom), 525th Military Police Battalion, grapples with a sailor during the Modern Army Combatives portion of the 2013 Army South Best Warrior Competition at Camp Bullis. The combatives program began in 1995 with the goal of preparing soldiers to close with and defeat the enemy in hand-to-hand combat. (DVIDS.)

Participants in the 8th Annual Fallen Defender rucksack march climb Three Bears Hill. This event honored Security Forces personnel killed in action since September 11, 2001. Participants included staff and students, local active and retired Security Forces personnel, and five Gold Star family members. Gold Star families are those who have lost a loved one in service to the nation. (DVIDS.)

In 2005, the officer in charge at Camp Bullis Training Site hosted a reunion for the Scheele family at the Scheele ranch house on the property, which the Army rented from Otto Scheele in 1917 and acquired in 1923. These three ladies are the surviving daughters of Otto Scheele. (FSHM.)

An Air Force staff sergeant coaches a southpaw gunner on the M240 general purpose machine gun. This belt-fed, gas-operated medium machine gun fires the 7.62-millimeter NATO cartridge and replaced the M60. In 1977, the Army adopted the M240 for use in vehicles and as a coaxial gun. It was later issued to the infantry. (DVIDS.)

Airmen 1st Class Neal Kiser and Miranda Gonzales unload boxes of machine gun ammunition for the 902nd Security Forces Squadron's machine gun training at Camp Bullis. Each box contains 800 rounds of linked 7.62-millimeter cartridges for the M240 machine guns. Without the logistical means to deliver sufficient ammunition, the guns would be dead weight. (DVIDS.)

S.Sgt. Javier Nunez, 353rd Special Operations Group, Kadena Air Base, Japan, leads a team to breach and clear a building during a special response team training exercise at the Combat Leadership Course. This team is moving in a "stack," a formation that provides security and firepower in all directions. (DVIDS.)

S.Sgt. Jacob Dipietro, 525th Military Police Battalion, checks his target at the M4 Carbine Zero Range during the 2013 Army South Best Warrior Competition at Camp Bullis. The purpose of zeroing the weapon is to adjust the sights so the point of impact of the rounds fired matches the aiming point. (DVIDS.)

Soldiers pass through the MOUT (Military Operations in Urban Terrain) site wearing the MILES gear. Troops may experience sniper fire, booby traps, or any of a dozen combat situations. Video cameras throughout the site record everything that happens. In an after-action review, the video is used to show what happened and to highlight the mistakes made and the tactically correct actions. (FSHM.)

A squad leader for the 277th Engineer Company (Horizontal) talks with two of his troops beside a dozer during a battle assembly weekend at Camp Bullis while the unit assembles its vehicles for an upcoming mission. The word "horizontal" in the unit designation means that it builds and maintains roads. (DVIDS.)

At the Camp Bullis MOUT Site, engineers from the 836th Engineer Company, a Texas Army National Guard outfit, prepare to lower a simulated casualty after a notional explosion in a building. The unit's mission is to respond to natural and man-made disasters to conduct search and extraction operations. (DVIDS.)

Sgt. Robert Gonzales, maintenance squad leader for the 277th Engineer Company (Horizontal) of San Antonio, Texas, and another soldier jump over a muddy trail after helping recover a vehicle from another unit that had become stuck in March 2015. Both soldiers are wearing the Army Combat Uniform with digital pattern camouflage. (DVIDS.)

First Lt. Chi Wing Pang (left) and Sfc. Stephen Eisele from Brooke Army Medical Center celebrate after winning the Regional Health Command–Central (Provisional) 2016 Best Medic Competition at Camp Bullis. The 72-hour competition tested each two-man team both physically and mentally. In the background is an M997 ambulance. (DVIDS.)

Soldiers from the 162nd Area Support Medical Company assist pilots transferring a patient from a UH-60 helicopter to a field hospital during Operation Papercut, an Army National Guard training exercise at Camp Bullis in 2014. This deployment training exercise involved air assault training, medical air and ground evacuation, and emergency medical treatment. (DVIDS.)

Sgts. Nicholas Santos, left, and Edwin Luchendo from the 1st Cavalry division rappel themselves and a simulated casualty down a 25-foot cliff in the northwest part of Camp Bullis during the Army's Best Medic Competition in 2016. Out of sight atop the cliff is the belay man controlling the descent of the casualty. (DVIDS.)

Physician assistants Maj. Latiba Cummings (right) and Spc. Megan Vinton, 162nd Area Support Medical Company, monitor a patient during Operation Papercut on Joint Base San Antonio–Camp Bullis. (DVIDS.)

S.Sgt. Kevin Brown assesses a simulated combat casualty during a tactical exercise at Camp Bullis as part of the 2016 Army Contracting Command's Best Warrior Competition. Brown is assigned to the 928th Contracting Battalion at Grafenwohr, Germany. (DVIDS.)

S.Sgts. Rayanne Osborne, left, Ken Roberts, center, and Dustin Tice, right, practice breaching and clearing buildings during special response team training while attending the Combat Leaders Course at Camp Bullis in September 2012. This course is a five-week class that teaches combat operations and leadership tactics to Security Forces members. (DVIDS.)

S.Sgt. Dustin Tice, 18th Security Forces Squadron, left, is the first man through the door as his team breaches a building during special response team training at Camp Bullis in 2012. The members of his "stack" will follow and cover him as they clear the room of hostiles. (DVIDS.)

Spc. Christina Laufer, assigned to US Army South's Headquarters Support Company, fires a burst on the M249 machine gun range in 2015. Soldiers participated in a four-part course of instruction that included a period of primary marksmanship instruction, a dry run-through of the engagement skills trainer, familiarization firing, and finally, the firing of the M249. (DVIDS.)

A soldier from US Army South's Operations Company of the Headquarters and Headquarters Battalion loads a belt of linked 5.56-millimeter ammunition into an M249 machine gun. This was part of an exercise to familiarize the troops with the M249 squad automatic weapon and its capabilities. Approximately 17 troops participated in the familiarization firing. (DVIDS.)

Sgt Marci DiOssi, assigned to the 102nd Training Division from Fort Leonard Wood, receives training on the M9 pistol from a fellow noncommissioned officer during the 80th Training Command's Best Warrior Competition at Camp Bullis in 2016. The competition is an annual event to identify the most-well-rounded soldiers. (DVIDS.)

First Lt. Chi Wing Pang, representing the Regional Health Command–Central, fires his M4 carbine during the US Army's Best Medic Competition at Camp Bullis in 2016. The M4 carbine is a shorter and lighter variant of the venerable 5.56-millimeter M16 rifle that was tested at Camp Bullis in 1965. (DVIDS.)

Sgt. Edwin Luchendo (front) and Sgt. Nicholas Santos, representing the 1st Cavalry Division at Fort Hood, move smartly away from the UH-60 Blackhawk medevac aircraft as it prepares to lift off with a casualty they had just uploaded during the US Army's Best Medic Competition at Camp Bullis in 2016. (DVIDS.)

Sgt. Marcy DiOssi of Fort Leonard Wood navigates the swing and jump obstacle at the obstacle course event during the 80th Training Command 2016 Best Warrior Competition. At this obstacle, each soldier must swing on the rope to the top of the rail, then jump to the ground. (DVIDS.)

Sfc. Daniel Aparicao of Fort Devens, Massachusetts, practices moving by bounds during the 80th Training Command 2016 Best Warrior Competition. Using this basic soldier skill, the soldier moves quickly from one covered position to the next, crouching with his weapon at the ready. This minimizes his exposure to enemy fire. (DVIDS.)

Spc. Scott Burgett, Headquarters and Headquarters Battalion, US Army South, tightens a second tourniquet while continuing to evaluate a casualty during the medical portion of the situational training exercise lanes at the battalion's field training exercise at Camp Bullis. Burgett wears the digital camouflage Army Combat Uniform, Kevlar vest, and helmet. (DVIDS.)

S.Sgt. Carlos Espada fires downrange during M16 qualification as part of the Army Contracting Command Best Warrior Competition in 2016. Espada is assigned to the 618th Contracting Team at Joint Base Elmendorf-Richardson, Alaska. (DVIDS.)

Soldiers from Headquarters and Headquarters Battalion, US Army South, complete the process of donning their protective masks, overgarments, boots, and gloves to get into Mission Oriented Protective Posture (MOPP) Level 4 during the chemical, biological, radiological, and nuclear portion of the situational training exercises during the battalion's field training exercise at Camp Bullis. (DVIDS.)

S.Sgt. Andreas Bond, from the Vermont Army National Guard and an instructor at the Army Mountain Warfare School, pulls himself forward through the horizontal rope obstacle using the "commando crawl" during the US Army's Best Medic Competition at Camp Bullis in 2016. This technique originated with the British Commandos in World War II. (DVIDS.)

After 100 years, the extensively modified original camp headquarters building still serves as the headquarters of Camp Bullis–Joint Base San Antonio. The signs around the shrubbery at left point out some of the history of the camp, such as the nearby prisoner-of-war compound and the headquarters itself. (FSHM.)

About the Organization

Preservation Fort Sam Houston, Inc., a 501(c)(3) private, nonprofit educational organization not affiliated with the Department of Defense, was established in 1984 to promote and support historic preservation at Fort Sam Houston and to support the activities of the Fort Sam Houston Museum. The organization participates with Fort Sam Houston in the preservation process as an interested party in the local community. It has pioneered the concept of the public-profit partnership for preservation projects on military installations. The organization renovated the historic Stilwell House for use as a venue for community events at Fort Sam Houston. By 1998, the building had been restored to its previous grandeur. Preservation Fort Sam Houston held a grand reopening of the Stilwell House. In 2013, the organization nominated Fort Sam Houston for a Richard H. Driehaus Preservation Award from the National Trust for Historic Preservation, recognizing Fort Sam Houston for its partnership in federal preservation. The award was presented on November 1, 2013. When Fort Sam Houston became part of Joint Base San Antonio, the organization expanded its horizon to the historic buildings on all of San Antonio's military bases. Today, Preservation Fort Sam Houston continues its historic preservation efforts and support for the Fort Sam Houston Museum.